Illuminated Journaling
Giving Creative Expression To Your Faith

Jann Gray

Lumenstar Publishing™, Inc.

Nashville, Tennessee

Jann Gray/Lumenstar Publishing, Inc
PO Box 24625
Nashville Tennessee 37202
www.LumenstarPublishing.com

Scripture quotations noted as ESV are from The Holy Bible, English Standard Version, copyright 2001 by Crossway, a publishing ministry of Good News Publishing

Scripture quotations noted as NIV are from The Holy Bible, New International Version, copyright 1973, 1978, 1984, 2011 by Biblica, Inc All rights reserved worldwide.

All artwork is the work of Jann Gray unless noted otherwise.

Library of Congress Cataloging-in-Publication Data

Illuminated Journaling/ Jann Gray. -- 1st ed.
ISBN 978-1-4951-6527-6

Dedication

To Jammy Jane
You taught me to tarry in the Word.

To my sister, Robyn
Your faith challenges me to love God more and
your friendship always helps me believe I can.

To Royce,
My quiet rock, problem solver and fellow dreamer.
So glad I stole your desk all those years ago!

To Weston,
In whom I see the promise of the Word.
You have filled my life with joy…and new vocabulary words!

I love you all—a bushel and a peck!

Acknowledgements

This book has been filling my heart almost from the moment that I opened my new Journaling Bible for the first time.

I have come to discover that the difference between what publishers mean when they say "this is a subject that needs our immediate attention" and what God means when He says, "I want you to give this your immediate attention" is about 18 months. As crazy as it may seem – I'm always going to go with the "God sized dreams option."

There are no words to adequately express my gratitude to all those who said, "Of course I will help!" Writing is a solitary activity that requires a crowd—and I am blessed to have the best crowd ever!

Royce B. Gray, you have smoothed out the path before I got there and allowed me to focus on what God wanted me to do next without the distractions of *obstacles*. You've got mad skills, Mr. Man.

John Driver – I don't know why other writers hate working with their editors. I've found the process of working through your edits to be a joy. You managed to find the balance between what publishing standards require and what needed to remain so that I didn't disappear! And here is the only math that ever made sense to me: Thank you x 1000 = not nearly enough!

Deborah Jackson, you have always challenged me with your love of learning and your attention to detail –what an amazing combination of skills you possess! I have been blessed to have had you apply both of these to your proof-reading – and the final manuscript is stronger because of it—thank you.

Tonya Gibbs, I've been inspired by your creativity from the moment I met you. Thanks for talking through the "creative" communication…you sharpened my thoughts.

John Luscombe and Doug McBain, is this really the first project we have worked on together? G.T. Luscombe is a great champion for Christian Resellers and you both are men of vision! Thank you for asking us to be a part of what you are doing…it's fun to work with "family!"

Dr. Vicky Black, I could not have done this without the haven you provided me at Hilltop B&B. You knew that the key to good writing was fruit smoothies, a place to stretch my legs, a pot of coffee, fresh veggies and a bit of human contact now and again. Thank you for your friendship and prayers.

Jeffrey "Pod" Holland…videographer and photographer extraordinaire! I'm not sure I know what the Podco XJ-74i does – but I sure am glad that it had the ability to make me look better than the Podco XJ-73e!

And how do I say thank you to my sweet sister, Robyn? God gifted me with the best Sister and Friend ever! I love you to the moon and back!

CONTENTS

Click

Every Bible I have ever owned has ended up being the repository of all sorts of evidence that I have met with God on the pages of His Word. If you were to do a quick flip through one of my Bibles, you would find that sermon notes, prayers, word studies and cross references have been scribbled in the margins and that words and even whole paragraphs have been underlined, circled and color coded. These marks on the pages of my Bibles were not put there to distract from the Word of God, but rather to remind me of the personal insights and instructions God has shared with me as I studied and meditated on His Word.

I have now begun to add a whole different type of "mark" into my newest Bible. It now also contains illustrations—a creative expression that I call *Illuminated Journaling*.

It was a moment my mother's heart wanted to remember forever. I stood a few yards behind them as Royce and Weston wandered down towards the beach to watch the sun sink below the waves. And just as casually as they had both turned towards the beach to get closer to the water, Weston put his arm up around his dad's shoulders and leaned in.

My heart filled up, as did my eyes. And then I did what any self-respecting mother would do—I pulled out my camera. (This was when my phone still "flipped" and didn't take pictures). The sun had set just enough that I needed to turn on my flash. **Click** and there in the viewfinder was the silhouette of my two guys leaning in towards each other . . . Dad and Son admiring the work of their Heavenly Father.

That photo sits on my desk. I love that by just glancing at it, I am transported back to that moment. It was the moment I knew we would all survive the teenage years. The moment I knew that Dad and Son were solid and united—ready to face whatever the future might hold.

We had no idea that the future held Royce needing a kidney transplant. No idea that there would be years of adjusting to the "new normal"—all while Weston was still a teenager. In the midst of so much that was *not* certain, that photo stood as a reminder that there was a moment when I *knew* that no matter what happened, Royce and Weston were ready to face it together. And I watched that moment of "knowing" turn into a season of surety—when Royce got his kidney transplant and Weston was there helping him each step along the way. They not only survived—they thrived. And my mother's heart was filled once again.

It was my love of photography and the way a picture can transport me back to the moment that a precious memory occurred, which led to my love of journaling in my Bible using words and images. I call this style of journaling *Illuminated Journaling* because like the flash of a camera, it captures the moments I have met with God on the pages of His Word and allows me to return to that meeting again and again—refreshing my memory and reinforcing the truths I have learned.

Illuminated Journaling allows me to capture my own picture—a *selfie* if you will—of myself with God while we stand together admiring the works of His hands. Sometimes the picture is of me before I knew what the future would hold. Sometimes it is of the celebration of seeing a task complete. Other times, it captures the moment when the truth finally sank in . . . and I "got it." Still others record the time I "missed it yet again."

As I flip through the pages of my Bible, I see where I've been, anticipate where He will lead me and I rejoice in His constancy, presence and love for me every day—every moment of my life. And if my fickle heart even *tries* to forget, I have the evidence right there on the pages of my Bible that He never forgets, never fails, never leaves and always *loves*. **Click** and there in the viewfinder of my *Illuminated Journal* is our silhouette . . . Him loving me and me loving Him right back.

CHAPTER ONE

The Elephant In The Room

"I believe God made me for a purpose, but He also made me fast. And when I run I feel His pleasure."

-- Eric Liddell, **Chariots of Fire**[1]

Before we begin, I must acknowledge that I see the elephant in the room . . . I'd have to be blind to miss him. So let's just deal with the question that is meandering around in the back of your mind, if not on the tip of your tongue.

It wasn't long after I started journaling in my Bible that I had the first of many friends send me an email that went something like this. I will add my running commentary in italicized brackets so you can know what I was thinking as I read it.

Hey Jann

I'm writing here, because I didn't know if I should leave my question on your blog. *[See, right there you can tell she is a friend, because most folks feel absolutely free to say or ask anything in the comment section of my blog.]*

I love what you shared today. Girl, I didn't know you could draw! [*Me either!*] I have to say that your journal entry[2] (is that what you call it) in your Bible touched my heart! Joseph does get the short end of the stick when it comes to the Christmas story and when you shared about your grandfather, the carpenter, and how you related something he used to do to what you thought might be true about Joseph, I found myself just nodding along with you. It sounds like both our grandfathers were really similar. I will never read the Christmas Story again without casting my own grandfather in the role of Joseph! [*Me too! I have such a vivid picture of what I think Joseph's hands looked like because I have watched my own grandfather's hands take a piece of wood and shape it into something useful. They weren't pretty hands, but they were gentle and skilled – much like I image Joseph's were.*]

Like I said, I really loved your blog post...but I just have to ask you...

Aren't you afraid that God is going to be mad at you for drawing in the Bible? It's His WORD*!* [*I imagined her saying those last three words in a bit of an elevated whisper, much like someone does when they are sharing unpleasant news or are nervous about gaining the attention of that elephant in the room.*] I am probably worrying too much about this and I know you will help me feel better about it, but I just had to ask.

Hugz, RT

So there it is, the elephant in the room[3]. *Illuminated Journaling* encourages you to write, draw, doodle, sketch, paint and stamp right on the pages of your Bible. And the thought of doing that might make you just a bit uncomfortable . . . or maybe *a lot* uncomfortable. In my enthusiasm to introduce you to joys of journaling in your Bible, I do not want to ignore what might be your biggest inhibition about it.

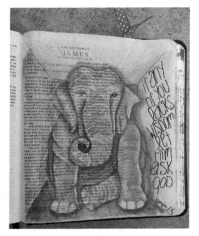

So let me be clear. I *love* the Word of God! I approach it with reverence and awe. I do not want to treat it lightly or with *any* disrespect. What I feel is okay for me may not feel right for everyone, and I do not think that I occupy the "enlightened" position here. But please, allow me to share with you some of the boundaries I have set for myself in this endeavor and describe a bit of the path I have walked in seeking for myself answers to these questions.

I ordered my *Journaling Bible* online and was waiting for it to arrive. I had done a couple of sketches and was trying to figure out what I wanted to do first,. But mostly, I was just excited to get started. I saw the box sitting on my porch as I pulled in the driveway and my heart actually started beating faster. You wouldn't believe how quickly I got the groceries put away so I could get into my studio and open up this treasure.

As I removed the wrapping and opened the cover for the first time, I was struck by how clean and pristine the pages were . . . and for the first time I acknowledged the unspoken question that had been lurking in the back of my mind. *"God if I start journaling in my Bible, are You going to consider this an act of irreverence . . . a defacing of Your Word? Or will You see what I am doing as my way of wanting to get to know You better and offer You a gift of praise with my heART?"*

I think everyone that wants to begin *Illuminated Journaling* needs to have this conversation with God and ask Him these questions personally. I hold God's Word in reverence. It is His message to met—how I get to know Him. I want to treat it respectfully. But I have also come to realize that the book that holds the *words* of God is much like the church building housing the *people* of God. Both should be taken care of and treated with respect, but we should never consider them holier than the actual words or people contained within.

Church looks different depending on the people who attend. Some churches are formal and some are more casual. Some use hymnals, while others sing worship songs from lyrics projected onto a screen. They may look very different, but underneath they serve the same purposes: *to reach people for Christ, disciple them in their faith and send the people of the church out into the world to be ambassadors for Christ*. Anything that does not detract from those *purposes* is simply *preference*.

I am blessed to own several Bibles. They too look different. I have some that I love to use for studying because they provide me with invaluable word study resources. Others are more for reading for comprehension—they use words that are easier for me to understand and look more like a chapter in a book without verse numbers. I have one Bible version that I take to church with me because my pastor uses a version that I have not used before, and I like being able to read along with him and not be distracted by the fact that my favorite Bible says it a little bit differently. They look different, but they all serve the same purpose—*to reveal God and His character to me, showing me how to live a holy and righteous life and making it clear my need for a Savior within God's plan for my salvation.* Again, anything that does not detract from that purpose is *preference.*

I have found that journaling *in* my Bible helps make the Word of God a living and breathing thing *inside* my heart. That is exactly what God wants His Word to do in my life, so my journaling is fulfilling the purpose of His Word. I'm not slopping paint on the page just to create art—I am approaching His Word reverently and recording what I have learned when I have met with Him on the pages of my Bible. I very intentionally have asked Him to reveal to me if He has *any* displeasure in what I am doing. I have not experienced a single check in my spirit. However, I do continue to occasionally bring the subject up again and ask Him to be the Guide of my work in my Bible. As a child of God, He has created me for a purpose and He also made me creative. I can honestly say that when I am working in my Bible, I feel His pleasure.

I think we should each ask the Lord how He feels about it. Does He feel like the time that you spend in the Word doing journaling is helping your relationship? Does He see it as an act of worship? Or does He feel that you are defacing His Word? And then listen. Not with a heart that thinks it knows the answers because of how we have "always" approached His Word—but rather with a heart that seeks to know if we have His approval to approach His Word in this manner.

If you feel that you have His permission to proceed, I must warn you that changing one's long-term thought processes is hard work, even when we know the change will be for our good. This seems especially true when we are older than twenty-one. We live most of our lives doing things because such is the way we have always done them—not necessarily because these ways are *more* right than others. If we are motivated to do something differently because we are convinced that it will benefit us, it is still difficult to change. This just means we have to be *intentional* about replacing the old behavior with the new. Research suggests that it takes about twenty-one days for new ideas and behaviors to become "natural" to us.

The 21-Day Experiment

If you feel that journaling in your Bible would be beneficial, consider embarking upon this 21 Day Experiment. For twenty-one days, pull out your bible every day and add something to it—just in the margins. It doesn't have to be fancy. Don't cover up anything unless you are comfortable doing so. Be certain to not skip a day. This exercise is about changing your way of thinking—the discipline of doing this everyday will help strengthen your commitment to it.

Each day before you begin, flip through the pages from the previous days and recall what you learned about the Lord while you were working on those pages. And each day before you begin, ask God to reveal Himself to you during your time together while you are journaling. If this new way of thinking about Bible Journaling is something the Lord approves of for you, I believe you will feel His pleasure. When we *know* that we have His approval, we can be less timid in our approach.

As you continue on in this book, you will find some journaling prompts at the end of each chapter. You can use these as a starting point on your *21-Day Experiment.*

I just took a quick peek, and is it just me, or is that elephant shrinking just a bit? Let's see if we can make him head on out to someone else's room and leave us alone completely!

You may just be embarking on your 21-day experiment, and that is the perfect time to make some additional choices regarding how you wish to approach *Illuminated Journaling* for yourself. My answers to these same questions have changed over time . . . and I expect yours will too. Mine changed because I learned more about my preferences through the process of working in my Bible. I was glad that I had thought through a few of my *preferences* because I used them as guidelines in the beginning.

Will this Bible be your primary Bible or will you use it as a separate tool for your study and devotional time?

There is no right answer for this one, but it is a choice that will determine the scope of some of your other choices. Many people want to have a single Bible for everything that they do, while others want the freedom to choose different Bibles for different activities. Both are perfectly reasonable options and the reasons for choosing either are as varied as the colors of the rainbow.

My preference is to keep this Bible as a separate resource for my devotional times. I use it solely as a place to respond to God after I have studied His Word with my other Bibles and reference books. That's what works for me, but I have dear friends whose eyes glaze over when I start talking about the different Bibles that I use for study, research, church, my women's Bible study and my *Illuminated Journaling.* To them, having a single Bible to turn to, regardless of the activity, makes the most sense to them as they like the consistency of having everything in one place.

My personal preference for using different Bibles was established long before I ever thought of journaling in my Bible. It is perhaps more a reflection of my age than anything else. Don't get me wrong, I *love* my tablet because I can have a gazillion different books on it and I no longer have to worry about my suitcase being overweight because of the books I take with me when I travel. However, when I am digging deep into the Word, I want to have physical books spread out around me.

There is no happier place for me than the middle of my bed with all of my various Bibles and reference books spread out around me as I study. I suppose someone who really loves cooking would feel similarly about being in their kitchen with all of their tools right at their fingertips. In that moment, it feels like the possibilities are endless. So, for me, adding another Bible into this mix was not a difficult choice. It is simply how God made me with my preferences. Your preferences are also a part of how He made you as well—and equally appropriate for Bible Journaling.

If you choose to use a single Bible for all of your activities, you may want to consider purchasing a Journaling Bible. The wider margins will give you more options for notes in addition to your *Illuminated Journaling* posts. I have chosen a specific Bible for my art journaling— the *English Standard Version Journaling Bible* (ESV). I am pretty sure that when Crossway published it, they were thinking more about giving people a larger margin to write in, but I have loved how versatile it is for note taking, traditional journaling and *Illuminated Journaling*. I also recommend it for new journalers because I have found the paper to be the most forgiving when I add liquid mediums (watercolor, clear gesso, etc.) onto its pages.

In the fall of 2014, it became almost impossible to find a wide margin Journaling Bible either in stores or online. Bible publishers may have not known *why* all their Journaling Bibles were being purchased, but they were quick to respond and now you can find a wide margin, Journaling Bible in just about any translation that you would wish to use. I have some information about several of the most popular versions in the Resource section at the end of the book. If you don't see your favorite version listed, don't despair—you may just need to do a little research or call the publisher.

I use this Bible as part of my daily quiet time and devotions . . . but it is *in addition* to my main study Bible. This helps me keep things a little clearer. Just as I have Bibles and study aids to help me gain a greater understanding of scripture, this Bible is a designated aid in my devotional process— specifically the part where I respond back to God.

Knowing how you intend to use your Bible will help you answer the next question.

Will your art be confined to the margins or will you use the entire page?

This is another great question, and the answer may change over time. My very first entries in my Bible[4] were ones that I made in the margin only or in an open area of a page at the end of a book. I was still working out my 21-Day Experiment and asking God if this journaling process was something He wanted me to incorporate into our

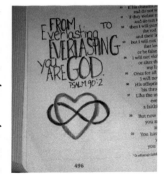

relationship in an ongoing manner. Thus I chose to stick to the margins until I heard from Him clearly. It was about day

eleven when I realized that what I wanted to communicate on the page couldn't be contained in the two inch margin[5]—and it was then that I knew God also wanted me to express myself as clearly as possible. If that meant using a full page or even several whole pages, I needed to do it to the best of my ability.

For me, I light on the side that says, "I'm not trying to keep this Bible pristine." My primary focus is what I have learned about Him and His love, plans, desires, commands and promises for me and His church. Those things are never neat, tidy or pristine when I am working them out with no art involved . . . so I expect there will be a bit of a mess when I add ink, paint, chalk and pencil into the mix. I have come to the conclusion, for myself, that because I have chosen to use a separate Bible for *Illuminated Journaling,* I can allow my art to spill over onto the printed words—and you need to decide this same issue for yourself.

I do want to add one other caveat. Paul spoke clearly to the Believers at the church in Corinth regarding their freedom. He said, *"Everything is permissible—but not everything is beneficial. Everything is permissible—but not everything is constructive. Nobody should seek his own good, but the good of others."* [6]

I believe I have the freedom to create posts that cover as much of the page as I need to effectively communicate what I am trying to say, but I am mindful of what I share publically. My Journaling Bible's primary purpose is to grow my relationship with my Heavenly Father—and to that end, I am free to express myself in whatever manner works best. But when I choose to take what I have done as a private expression to God and share it publically, I have another layer of responsibility to take into consideration.

When I post onto my Facebook™ page, Instagram™ or in a Bible Journaling group, I am careful to share things that will encourage people in their walk, not cause them to stumble. Most of the people who see my work in a public forum are seeing art on the pages of my Bible, not the context of why I believe it is all right for me to add art there. They still see the elephant in the room and unlike my friend who sent me an email; they will probably never ask me why I think it is okay. If the art I share hinders their relationship with God or my ability to share Christ with them in any way, it would be better for me not to share it. It is permissible, but not constructive. Therefore, I choose to adapt my techniques on these pages to ensure that most, if not all, of the words on the page are still visible.

Finally, I have one more guideline I use when I sit down to journal. *I do not add art into my Journaling Bible just for the sake of "art."* I have other journals for that. If I add it to my Bible, it has to pass my personal "*is this where it belongs*" test. I'm not saying that every thing I add has to be earth shattering or eternally profound, but I only want to add things that further my understanding and relationship with God.

It is a simple question to ask—and so far, the choices have been pretty clear. I am glad I have other journals where I can put things that are not right for my Journaling Bible. The fact that it doesn't need to live on the pages of my Bible doesn't mean that it doesn't have value. I am just trying to find my way along the path that leads to me fulfilling God's purpose for me and feeling His pleasure. I know you want that too.

Illuminations and **Click Stops**

In my experience, I incorporate new ideas into my life by actually trying them for myself. As we move together through this book, it is my desire to help you discover if *Illuminated Journaling* would be a helpful practice in your ongoing relationship with the Lord. To that end, I will be adding two additional elements to each of the chapters: ***Illuminations*** and ***Click** Stops*.

Illuminations will be short sections with questions for you to consider. If you are working through *Illuminated Journaling* with a group, these could be used for group discussion. But they are really here to help you approach the topic of the chapter in a more tangible way rather than merely observing it from far off.

***Click** Stops* will be journaling prompts designed to help you tighten your focus on what you may want to add to your *Journaling Bible*. Like I shared in the *Introduction*, part of what *Illuminated Journaling* does for me is to capture a snapshot of where I am at in the moment. Some of my entries really do represent a type of selfie. But others also focus on my understanding of God or my praise and worship of Him. It really varies. Regardless of what the purpose of the entry is going to be, I go through a process of taking the insights I have gained in my study and thinking through how I can visually represent them.

I hope you will stop now and work your way through the ***Illuminations*** and ***Click** Stop* for chapter one. You may want to write in a designated journal or here in your book. Later, you can determine what you may want to add into your *Journaling Bible*. Or you can forge bravely ahead and dive into journaling in your Bible right now . . . it's totally up to you and God!

Illumination

If you have never watched the movie, **Chariots of Fire**, let me recommend that you do so soon. And if you have, you might want to watch it again.

Eric Liddell was a man who loved God first and running second. He qualified for Great Britain's Men's Track and Field team for the 1924 Olympics in Paris. However, when the qualifying heats for his favored distance of 100 meters were held on a Sunday, he refused to run. Even when pressured by the Olympic committee, he simply would not run on the day he considered to be God's proclaimed day of rest. Because the qualifying heats for the 400-meter race were held the next day, Liddell was still able to compete in the Olympics—and though he had never won a 400-meter race before that day, he took home the gold.

Afterwards, he was swarmed by the press who wanted to know more about his faith and why he would allow it to control his participation in the Olympics.

He shared:

> *You came to see a race today. To see someone win. It happened to be me. But I want you to do more than just watch a race. I want you to take part in it. I want to compare faith to running in a race. It's hard. It requires concentration of will, energy of soul. You experience elation when the winner breaks the tape—especially if you've got a bet on it. But how long does that last? You go home. Maybe your dinner's burnt. Maybe you haven't got a job. So who am I to say, "Believe, have faith,"*

in the face of life's realities? I would like to give you something more permanent, but I can only point the way. I have no formula for winning the race. Everyone runs in her own way, or his own way. And where does the power come from, to see the race to its end? From within. Jesus said, "Behold, the Kingdom of God is within you. If with all your hearts, you truly seek me, you shall ever surely find me." If you commit yourself to the love of Christ, then that is how you run a straight race.

I believe God made me for a purpose, but he also made me fast. And when I run I feel His pleasure.[7]

Have you thought about what God's purpose is for your life? Write it here:

Describe a time when you felt God's pleasure in something that you were doing. Knowing what that feeling is like will help you determine if you are feeling His pleasure when you spend time journaling in your Bible.

Are you considering doing the *Illuminated Journaling 21-Day Experiment*? Try using the **Click** Stop prompt as your first journaling Bible entry.

Click Stop

Take a look at what you wrote on the second *Illuminations* question. Read Philippians 2:13. What does this verse say gives God pleasure?

How might this verse impact *Illuminated Journaling* for you?

Describe what the picture would look like you could just pick up a camera and **click** it. In other words, what would it look like to capture what you want to express to God about His Word, your reverence for it and your desire for Him to find pleasure in your gift.

Here is my entry[8] – I had to turn the page because both pages near the verse already had entries on them. Sometimes

it just works out that way. I could have also just worked on my entry in a sketchbook and taped it in as a tip in. There is no right or wrong answer, so when you find yourself with *more journaling and less page*, feel free to do what works best for you.

Do a quick sketch of it on scratch paper. You can use the Margin Templates in the Resource Section or work in a separate Journal.

If you are comfortable, take your sketch (it may just be a quote or a phrase in addition to an image) and add it into the margin of your Journaling Bible near Philippians 2:13. This entry can be a reminder of how God answered you when you asked if He would find pleasure in your journaling in your Bible.

CHAPTER TWO

See And Remember

"Jann! Don't forget your books!"

I'm sure my mother must have said that sentence a hundred times as I was headed out the door to school. Now, in my defense, we didn't have backpacks when I was in elementary school and I've never really been a morning person. My whole elementary education would have been an entirely different experience had I had a backpack and a Starbucks near my house!

But alas, we didn't. So my poor mother inevitably found herself calling to me as I was halfway down the sidewalk from our house,

"Jann! Don't forget your books!"

My Mom was a smart lady and a terrific problem solver. She clearly knew the day would come when she wouldn't be there to remind me to take my computer when I headed out the door to work. And in her defense, she didn't know the incredible role coffee would play in helping me to become a fully functional adult before 8:00 am. So she came up with another solution. Each night, she would place my books on the small shelf next to the front door. My Mom was the one who introduced me to the principle of *See And Remember.*

When we really need to remember something, we ought not rely just on our ability to pluck the memory out of thin air. The *See And Remember Principle* says: if you want to be sure and remember something, leave yourself a *visual reminder*.

The inventor of *Post-It Notes* clearly understood the *See And Remember Principle*, and I rise up and call him blessed several times a week for creating such a life-changing product. My refrigerator and daily planner are filled with grocery lists, errand lists and to do lists on multicolored "stick-able" squares of paper.

I hate making more than one trip to the grocery store, so I have a sticky note pad attached to my refrigerator. I add items to it throughout the week when I notice I have run out of something or I decide to try a new dish that requires an ingredient I don't already have. Rather than trying to keep that ever-changing list sorted out in my head , this is a much better way to ensure I get what I need. An aimless, nomadic journey through the grocery aisle is not the time, nor the place, to be playing the "memory" game. I will inevitably forget at least one or more items on the list. But when I use my visual list, I suddenly have excellent recall . . . and if it can help me with something as insignificant as a grocery list, I know it can help me be mindful of the spiritual truths God has taught me.

Experts who study how the brain works tell us that memory is one of the most perplexing and complicated functions of our cognitive framework. They don't understand exactly how we create a memory, but they do know that it is not all tied up neatly in one place. I've often joked that I need a better filing system in my head so I can remember things more easily. However, these experts would say that my memory of a single event isn't actually located in one file folder in my brain. In fact, it may actually reside in lots of different file folders—in bits and pieces—until I need the memory. Then my brain goes to work pulling those bits and pieces from their respective locations and putting them back together into a coherent memory. The more we can help our brain find those various folders, the better our memory is going to be.

Clearly, God knows better than any expert. As our Creator, He knows just how *fearfully and wonderfully made*[9] we truly are. He understands the complexity of our memories and knows precisely how they works. He is the originator of the *See And Remember Principle*.

God Uses the *See And Remember Principle* To Continually Reveal Himself To Us

There are so many things in nature and the world around us that God uses to tie a string around our finger, reminding us in very tangible ways that He is always there for us. Those things may be different for each of us, but as Paul wrote to the Romans, *"For what can be known about God is plain to them, because God has shown it to them. His invisible attributes, namely, his eternal power and divine nature, have been clearly perceived, ever since the creation of the world, in the things that have been made."*[10]

I love looking at the stars. I always have . . . even as a little girl. Early one summer evening, just as the brightest stars were beginning to reveal their distant twinkles amid twilight, my Mom had laid a blanket out in the backyard so we could lie down on it to stare up at the night sky. We had been there for a little while and before it had become dark enough for the stars to appear, we had been watching fireflies blink on and off. To me, they must have looked like stars as well because I said to my Mom, *"I know why God gave us fireflies."* I'm sure my Mom had to bite her lip to keep from laughing at my four-year-old certainty. *"Jann, why do you think God gave us fireflies?"* she asked. *"Well, stars are beautiful—but they are so far away. God wanted us to have twinkly things closer to us so we would be reminded that He is close by."* Not bad for a four-year-old theologian!

God's desire is not to remain an inaccessible mystery to us, so He chose to put things around us to help us know Him better . . . and He did so in such a way that we can at least begin to access the mystery without having to read the Bible. Yes, His Word is the ultimate place where the mystery becomes life within us, but He draws us with an infinite number of other variables. He's right there in the day-to-day details of the world, as we know it. We *see* the things that He has made and we *remember* Him.

The *See And Remember Principle* Helps Us Remember The Truths God Has Taught Us And The Things He Has Done For Us

In Genesis[11], God used the rainbow to remind us of His covenant that *"never again would all flesh be wiped off the face of the earth by flood."* I cannot imagine how Noah's family must have felt as they stepped off the ark and onto dry land for the first time after the flood. Grateful? Surely so. But no doubt they also were fearful and not at all fond of seeing clouds darken the sky.

This is because the *See And Remember Principle* works in the negative too! I'm sure the first time they saw clouds thicken in preparation for a thunderstorm, their memory kicked in to overdrive and they wanted to sprint back to the ark, just to be safe.

Dark clouds reminded them of the unending rain and destruction that had come to the earth the last time those clouds gathered in mass. The children may have thought of their friends that were no longer alive when they returned to dry land. The mothers may have thought of their homes that had been destroyed and all that was lost that was familiar and precious to them. The dads may have seen the clouds and remembered the feelings of helplessness that overpowered them when the rains began and they could only run to the shelter of the ark to protect their family.

Those dark clouds provoked strong memories and none of them were good.

God is so very compassionate. He knew the sight of those clouds might cause Noah and his family to be fearful. He knew that perhaps the sight would cause them to be afraid specifically of Him, not just the rain—even though He had provided a way out and spared their lives. And He knew that this fear could be passed on for generations to come. So He set the rainbow in the sky and told them, *"see it and remember the covenant I have made with you."*[12] He intentionally put the sign of His promise next to the very thing that caused them fear.

In the scriptures, God often used things we would *see* as a sign to *remember* the things He has done.

Illuminated Journaling Applies The See And Remember Principle To Our Study Of God's Word

Imagery is compelling. Even before we master reading and writing, we draw and doodle. There seems to be an innate desire within us to capture elements of our lives in an image format. Be it cave drawings, a stick figure family drawn by a child, a snapshot by a photo journalist or an oil painting crafted by a master, they each seek to create a visual representation of the life experience of the artist.

Illuminated Journaling taps into our emotions

Even the simplest painting or picture can evoke a strong emotional response. You probably don't even have to scroll down in your Facebook feed to find an image that you connect with on a visceral level. One that stopped me in my

tracks recently was the photo of a dog lying near the foot of his Navy Seal owner's casket during the soldier's funeral.[13]

I have several friends that have lost sons, brothers or spouses during the wars in Iraq and Afghanistan and for some reason, this picture instantly put me in touch with their painful loss. To this dog, his friend was just gone. No explanation of why he was gone was going to take away the loss. That picture helped me to reach out to my friends in a more compassionate way—

to identify just how profound the loss was for them. Imagery sometimes communicates more than words ever could.

When I add imagery to my Bible, there are times when the creative process can be even more satisfying than writing notes in the margin. Sometimes the imagery seems to find a way to communicate more accurately what I feel about God

and what I want to remember . . . it does so in a way that words alone could never do.

My journal entry called "Yesterday Ended Last Night,"[14] is one of those entries for me. For several days during my quiet time, I had felt the Lord pressing me regarding the amount of things I "carry over" from one day into the next. I had been drawn to Lamentations for several days in a row. Don't ask me why . . . nobody *wants* to hang out in Lamentations, for goodness sake! But apparently, that is where God felt we could do the most good with our time together.

As I read the familiar words, *"The steadfast love of the Lord never ceases, his mercies never come to an end; they are new every morning; great is your faithfulness,"*[15] I felt I must have been missing the point.

I tried repeating the words back to Him during my prayers. *"Lord, I know that your love never ceases. I'm sure of it. I count on it every day. I know I can't use up your mercies. My need is never going to be bigger than your capacity to fulfill it. Thank You!"* And still I didn't feel the freedom to move on to another verse or topic.

So we stayed there . . . to the point that I was beginning to lament my own inability to grasp what it was that I still wasn't grasping from this passage.

Then on Saturday night, we were visiting Joy Church International in Mt. Juliet, Tennessee. As I glanced at the title of the sermon listed in the bulletin, I was intrigued. Pastor Jim Frease was going to be speaking on the topic: *Yesterday Ended Last Night*. Little did I know that I was going to be a human puddle by the time we left the sanctuary. His sermon tied Philippians 3:13, 14 together with the same verses in Lamentations I had been focused on for several days.

After reading the verses in Lamentations, he turned to Philippians and read, " . . . *forgetting what lies behind and straining forward to what lies ahead, I press on toward the goal for the prize of the upward call of God in Christ Jesus.*"[16] He said, *"Too many of us forget that yesterday ended last night! God gives us a new start every day. He gives us new mercies every day. But too often we try to use today's mercies for yesterday's problems!"* I was so glad he didn't ask us to raise our hands if we knew he was speaking to us.

I know Pastor Frease probably shared many other truths during that sermon, but I confess that I don't remember even one of them. It was as if the last puzzle piece from a thousand-piece jigsaw puzzle had just fallen into place for me. Now I understood what God had been trying to get me to grasp during our camping trip in Lamentations!

Yes, His mercies *are* new every morning, but I kept hauling all the things I thought were unsettled from yesterday into today and He wanted it to stop. They were only unsettled in my mind—not His. The *"to do"* list from yesterday that hadn't gotten *"ta-done"* was now yesterday's news.

He wasn't saying that those things weren't going to need to be addressed today, only that I was bringing more than the list with me into the new day. I brought the worry. I brought the concern for how *I* was going to get it done today when I couldn't seem to get it accomplished yesterday.

My bet is that you may have done this too. Maybe you have tried to figure out how to use today's mercies for yesterday's problems . . . only to learn that we can't! Oh, we might manage for a day or two, but pretty soon the load just gets to be too heavy to bear—and eventually, we start giving God the *stink eye* because we think He is ignoring all that is weighing us down. Sound familiar?

My heart just broke as I realized that my refusal to leave yesterday's troubles behind and focus on what the Lord had for me today had become a stumbling block in our relationship. I tried not to make a scene during the service, but tears dripped from my eyes onto the pages of my bible.

I confessed my stubborn sin to God and asked Him to forgive me. I rejoiced that today was a new day, and I told Him that I trusted Him to deal with any unfinished business in His way, not mine. I was available if He wanted to use me—but I no longer wanted to act like the responsibility was mine to figure it out.

It was as if a huge weight had been lifted off my shoulders and because it had been such a hard lesson to grasp, I really wanted to capture it as quickly as possible.

When I got home, I went straight to my studio and began to work on my journal entry. I was kind of surprised that I didn't feel drawn to put this entry on the pages of the Lamentation verses, but I was so honed in on *"forgetting what lies behind, I press on"* part of this lesson, I felt it really belonged in Philippians. I closed my eyes to focus on what sort of image conveyed all of this insight to me.

It wasn't just the words from the verses. The impact of the lesson had come from the combination of the two passages *and* Pastor Frease's simple statement, "yesterday ended last night."

The picture that came to mind was of a sunrise coming up over the mountains. I'm pretty sure that part of the image was based on David's words in Psalms, *"I lift up my eyes to the hills, where does my help come from? My help comes from the LORD who made heaven and earth"*[17], but it also could have been from *The Sound of Music.*

Maria quoted David's Psalm as part of the reason she was not afraid to be alone in the mountains and I have often identified with the bad reputation she had for being a troublemaker when she was simply seeking to be authentic in her relationship with God. But I digress!

I quickly sketched the tops of the mountains and the outline of the silhouette of a person. In all honesty, I intended the silhouette to be me . . . but it looked more like a guy, and that was okay. For me *Illuminated Journaling* isn't about creating fine art, it is about capturing the fullness of my "heART."

I added some washes of color with watercolor paints and a bit more detail with colored pencils. I placed a title on the page, using the sermon title that had been instrumental to gaining this insight, I copied a portion of the Philippians passage to the bottom edge of the page and I called it done.

I did not need to do more journaling. The image immediately brought every aspect of this lesson to mind when I looked at it. Now every time I turn past this page in my Journaling Bible, I see it and the lesson is reinforced in my memory and my heart.

Illuminated Journaling brings the past into the present.

Images have the ability to transport us back to a moment in time and remind us of the details of that moment like it happened yesterday. It brings the past into the present. It brings a spiritual lesson to the forefront of our memory and refreshes our minds and hearts.

Something really remarkable happens when we engage imagery with our time in the Word. When we take the time to express what we have learned in a tangible way— with words and images—it is like the flash of the camera casting illumination on the subject and recording that particular moment in time in a way that ensures our ability to return to this truth time and again. We don't have to re-learn the truth; we can recall it and if need be, recommit to making it part of our daily walk.

After God delivered the Israelites from slavery in Egypt, you would have thought they would have plenty of things available to them to remind them of God's care and protection. But the truth is, they were no different than you and I . . . and unfortunately, they had a bit of a *"what have you done for me lately"* attitude when it came to recalling God's goodness.

To counteract this attitude, when God parted the waters of the Jordan river so that Joshua could lead the Israelites into

the Promised Land[18], God instructed them to take twelve stones from the dry riverbed of the Jordan and stack them up so that *"When your children ask, 'What do these stones mean to You?' Tell them, 'They are a memorial to what the Lord has done.'"*

I have placed an image of the stacked stones in my own Bible to remind me of this principle. Sometimes the lessons I learn when I meet with God on the pages of my Bible aren't profound and new. But particularly for those lessons I seem to need to return to again and again, I try to mark them with an entry in my Journaling Bible so they will stand as my own reminder—my personal *stones of remembrance*. Their presence reminds me of the things the LORD has done for me . . . and those images help translate the past lesson back into my present experience.

Illuminated Journaling helps us hide God's Word in our hearts.

Imagery is a powerful memory and study tool, and the process of creating it can add to our ability to retain the information and recall it more easily.

Recently, I had an opportunity to teach *Illuminated Journaling* to a group of girls at a Christian school. It was a concentrated inter-session class (between their semesters) that met for several hours each day. The girls had chosen my class as their elective for the week and were enthusiastic participants as we made *DIY Prayer Journals* and began helping them add journal entries into their journaling Bibles. It was one of the most enjoyable and rewarding weeks I have ever spent in a classroom.

One of the things I like to do with people who are new to *Illuminated Journaling* is to ask them to consider using one of their favorite verses to begin. I suggest this because they already have a strong connection to that verse. They probably already know exactly why it speaks to them in such a significant way and that means they can easily figure out a creative way to represent that in their Bible. When trying something new, it helps to start with something familiar as it provides a counterbalance for all the awkward and unfamiliar stuff that comes from acquiring a new skill.

So while we were elbow deep in glue and paper, I asked the girls to tell me what verse they had decided to use for their first *Illuminated Journaling* entry.

The first girl shared her verse—I kind of recognized it, but I think she may have been quoting from the *Teenagers Revised Standard Version* of the Bible. We talked for a bit as a group about how she could illustrate this verse in her Bible.

Then I asked another girl to share which verse she was going to use. She said, *"Oh . . . can I go grab my backpack? I didn't know we needed it with us at the table."* Several other girls spoke up and said that they too would need to retrieve their backpacks if we were going to talk about their favorite verse.

Like me, you may be somewhat horrified that so few of the girls could recall their favorite verses from memory. I have found in moments like this that it is best to hide the horrified judgmental attitude that is threatening to make my head spin like a top and instead find a way to make it a teachable moment. But watch out! The one you may end up teaching could be *yourself*!

I casually asked (beware: teenagers have an especially keen radar that alerts them to any adult's casual question), *"How many of you would say that you regularly memorize scripture as part of your personal Bible Study?"*

Okay, I suppose you don't really need a great radar system to spot where I was going with that question.

I should not have been surprised that their answers were a bit defensive. Even so, I was glad that they stuck with me and gave me a chance to redeem my blatant attempt to play the Holy Spirit in their lives. Sometimes I seem to subconsciously think that I should help Him out . . . after all, He is very busy, right? So if I notice something that isn't quite right, I have a hard time resisting the unwise urge to nudge the offender back into line. I'm still learning on this one.

One of the girls asked me, *"How much of the Bible do you have memorized?"* I wasn't sure how to respond. *"I'm not exactly sure,"* I said. *"I haven't kept track of the number of actual verses, but I have a pretty good amount memorized, I think."* The girls began their own discussion of how to figure out what constituted "a pretty good amount."

The final conclusion was that a pretty good amount could be quantified in one of two ways. First, if I could recall a verse from every book in the Bible, they would grant me said "pretty good amount" status.

Or, as a backup, if they could pitch me topic after topic and I could share a pertinent verse for each one until they couldn't think of any more to ask, I would have proven that I indeed had memorized a "pretty good amount" of the Bible. Honestly, I didn't want to touch the second option—I am long removed from topics that a teenage girl might be able to come up with. That made me a bit nervous, so I opted for working my way through all the books of the Bible while they continued working on their prayer journals.

Things moved along at a good clip until we got to *Ecclesiastes*. From the start, I had been thinking a couple of books ahead trying to make sure I was ready . . . and honestly, my brain was nervously processing how to deal with the *Song of Solomon*. I had already decided I was going to use chapter three in *Ecclesiastes* as the source for my verse from that book. I started in, *"There is a time for everything and a season for every matter under heaven: a time to be born, and a time to die; a time to plant and a time to pluck up what was planted . . .."*

The girls couldn't help giggling at the phrase "pluck up what was planted." Apparently their amusement was divided between using the words "pluck up" instead of "dig up" and the whole idea that there might have been a period of time actually designated for digging up the things you worked so hard to put in the ground.

I was still only half listening because I hadn't settled on an appropriate verse for *Song of Solomon*, so I continued bravely on. But I came back to *fully present* mode when one of the girls stopped the process by saying, *"Hey, wait a minute! That's not a Bible verse—that's a song!"*

And while I staunchly defended my choice of verse, none of the girls were buying it—they were absolutely convinced that I had confused a song for a scripture passage. Dear reader, don't roll your eyes! Have you never been surprised to find the words to a familiar song there on the pages of your Bible? I certainly have—and I try to remember to ask the Lord to bless the songwriter who helped me add more of my Bible into my memory.

To keep from totally losing control of the classroom, I suggested that we grab one of our Bibles and check it out. The girl with the least amount of glue on her hands ran to the sink to rinse off. She found the nearest Bible and turned to *Ecclesiastes*.

I was both vindicated and a bit mortified when she read the verses aloud. Indeed, *Ecclesiastes* chapter three contained the words to both a Biblical poem and an old song[19]—but what the girls immediately noticed was that the version I was quoting from bore little resemblance to what was in their *Journaling Bible*. They did give me credit, but the whole experience raised a question in my mind that I chose to deal with later that night.

After dinner, I decided to see if what I had begun to suspect during our class was actually true . . . and it was. Most of the scripture I had been quoting was from a version of the Bible that I had not used for more than thirty years! And the truth hit me: for quite some time, I had not been diligent about committing scripture to memory.

I was blessed as a child and young adult to be involved in Sunday School and Bible studies that encouraged regular memorization of the Bible, but clearly as I had gotten older, I had slacked off. I had probably been giving age too much credit for making it difficult to do.

I purposed in my heart to begin to add new scripture memory into my regular Bible Study time. Not to give myself an excuse, but *it is* harder to memorize now than it was when I was a kid. Those brain experts would probably say something really technical that actually means, *"use it or lose it."* Memories are formed along pathways. Much like wild animals wear a path in the woods between where they feed and sleep and get their water, our brains apparently create channels that make saving and recalling memories easier. If we haven't walked that path in a while, it's a bit more difficult to cut through the underbrush.

An unexpected blessing of *Illuminated Journaling* has been that I have added a significant amount of new scriptures into my memory vault. The time I spend working on an illustration or designing the lettering is time that I am focused on the scripture at hand. I refer back to it often during my work and that repeated reference has the effect of clearing a pathway between my short-term memory of the verses and the long-term memorization of them. That pathway leads to better recall—and is not nearly as frustrating as the flashcard method with my "older" brain.

I do have to share one more snippet from my time with the girls. Apparently, when I decided to stop playing Holy Spirit, He actually had a chance to work in the hearts of the girls. When I got to class the next morning, several of them were waiting to share their favorite verse with me . . . *from memory*! He is so good, isn't He?

Illumination

Do you have a favorite verse? A "life verse," perhaps? Write it here: *(You don't have to write from memory . . . that may happen naturally if/when you decide to create an entry in your Journaling Bible.)*

Why is this verse your favorite or important to you?

Is there a life experience you associate with it? Write it here: *(If this is an intensely personal experience, feel free to be discreet. You need not use names. Only write what you are comfortable committing to paper. One of the benefits of Illuminated Journaling is that we can document our feelings without giving away the details to a casual viewer).*

Click Stop

Take a look at both the passage of scripture you have written out in the *Illumination* section and the two follow-up questions. Is there something there that could be captured with an image?

Describe what that image might look like if you could just pick up a camera and **click** it. *Don't discard an idea because you wouldn't know how to draw it. We'll deal with some ideas a bit later of how to capture that image even with limited drawing skills.*

Better yet, try a quick sketch of it. Use a Margin Template in the Resource Section or work in a separate journal. *You may choose to use the full page at some point, but let's keep it as uncomplicated as possible for now.*

I'm serious. Put the book down and go get a pencil and an eraser. We aren't creating fine art here. Stick people will do . . . but don't limit yourself by what you think your capacity currently is. You may find, as I did, that when you begin working on these journal entries, you have skills you didn't know you possessed. Be open. Just try. Now go sketch what this verse means to you and I'll meet you back here in Chapter Three.

Embracing God's Word With All Of Your Mind

Jesus certainly knew what it would take for us to be in right relationship with Him. I think it is significant that when asked what He considered the greatest commandment, Jesus responded with, *"to love the Lord your God with all your heart, all your soul and all your mind."*[20] Why did he choose these three areas?

Have you ever heard people refer to themselves as "right-brained" or "left-brained" thinkers? According to the theory of left-brain or right-brain dominance, each side of the brain

controls different types of cognitive functioning. People supposedly prefer one type of thinking to the other. A left-brained person is thought to be more logical, analytical and objective, while a right-brained person is thought to be more intuitive, thoughtful and subjective. However, recent medical and psychological research has suggested that it may not be quite as simple as having a predisposition to one type of thinking over the other.

To tell you the truth, I'm not so sure I like the sound of that—why can't it just be that simple, for Pete's sake?

For many years, I have felt quite comfortable defining myself "left-brained with a creative bent." Although I am adopted and my adoptive parents were not around when I said my first words, you would never have convinced them that my first word was anything other than the word, "Why?" To this day, life would be torturous if I couldn't ask my favorite question. Maybe you can relate.

If Jesus wasn't encouraging analytically bent people to approach God with their creative self and *vice a versa,* what could He have meant when He told us to *"love the Lord with all your mind?"*

While there are still many mysteries as to how the brain functions, experts now say that what once was described as being *predisposed* to use either the left or right hemisphere of their brain should now more accurately be thought of in terms of actions being a *reflection of their repetitive processes.* Ah, that really simplified the matter, yes? Oh good grief! Can't we just keep saying we're left-brained or right brained?

Let it go, man. Let it go.

Let's think of your brain as a thickly wooded forest where no one has ever set foot. One day a tribe of hunters settles near the forest and ventures into the woods in search of food. At first, it is slow going. They have to be careful not to get lost and forward motion more than a few feet at a time is very difficult due to the dense underbrush. But, over time, they begin to wear paths to their favorite hunting spots. Then another path to where they have found the clearest water.

And yet another to where the bees have hidden their sweetest honey.

As they return again and again to the places that have rewarded their efforts, they no longer have to work so hard to get there because they have worn pathways that keep the entangling brush out of their way. These paths make doing the things they need to do every day more efficient and they cannot imagine their life being any better.

But if you were to get a bird's eye view of the forest and their pathways, you would be dumbstruck by all the places they have missed because they quit exploring once they met all of their immediate needs. They had gotten comfortable with the familiar paths. You would see the amazing waterfall that was ice cold and so much more refreshing than the stream from which they currently get their water. You would see that one of their most commonly walked paths passes right by a clearing where all kinds of plants and animals live that would be really helpful to them—if they only knew it was there.

But they don't know. They keep returning to the same places along the same paths. Nothing wrong with those paths—but if they could just be motivated to explore a bit more, their lives would move from good to great.

I think that is what Jesus is talking about when He said that we should love the Lord with *all* of our minds. We need to keep exploring. Keep searching to find those hidden treasures in our brains that will allow us to know Him better, love Him more and serve Him with all of the gifts and abilities He placed in us when He gave us life.

Not long after I began journaling in my Bible, I had a bit of an "aha" moment regarding this commandment. I've begun to see that when it comes to Bible study, I have defaulted to that part of my brain that is in my comfort zone or on the path of least resistance for thinking and solving problems . . . and that means I am missing something significant in regards to how well I can know, love and serve God.

Knowing that is happening is one thing . . . changing it is another thing altogether.

If I am going to create new pathways for my brain, I am going to have to be intentional about *not* choosing my favorite paths. I need to find a way to get out of my comfort zone . . . doing Bible Study differently so I can begin to forge new pathways to these yet undiscovered treasure troves. Jesus knows they are there and He is urging me to become an adventurous Bible student once again.

Yes, *once again*. When we were younger, we were better at being explorers. We didn't seem to mind so much that it took work to clear away the overgrowth and find the treasure. It was an adventure worth jumping into with both feet.

And remember, it isn't just getting tired of the work that has inhibited us from continually forging new paths in our brains. Most of us, from a young age have been told what we *were* good at and unfortunately, what we *were not* so good at too. Even the label of being left-brained or right-brained can quench our desire to explore and see what else we could if only we would venture out and try.

I came across a box of my old report cards while we were cleaning out my Mom's house preparing it for sale. I found it fascinating that even in high school, many of the teachers wrote notes to my parents—and most were very encouraging letting my parents know about improvement I had made or areas I could do better in with more effort. However, one of my freshman report cards contained a note from my art teacher that read, "*Mrs. Saulsberry. It is a good thing that you have enrolled Jann in band as she does not have a creative bone in her body.*"

Well that's a fine thing to say!

I don't remember reading that note, but I'm sure that I did because we were handed two copies of our report cards at the end of the school day and were told to get our parents to sign one copy and return it. I'm sure her words stung because I remember enjoying "art" up to that point. And while that note was just one person's opinion, I apparently put more stock in it than I should have because I do know I did not enroll in any more art classes—and for most of my life, I limited my creative expression to "crafty DIY" kinds of projects.

Let me hasten to say that I do not hold my ninth grade art teacher responsible for my choices to not create pathways in my brain that led to a more refined artistic skill set. Nor do I think that if she had only encouraged me, my ability would have rivaled Michelangelo! But I do think we begin to forge those "comfortable" pathways at a pretty young age—and unless we are encouraged to keep exploring and perfecting additional skills, we begin to limit the things we attempt. Before long, we seem to predominantly use one part of our brain more than the other.

I have come to believe that saying "I'm left-brained" is *descriptive, not diagnostic.* Yes, I use the skills that emerge from the left side of my brain with greater efficiency, but that does not mean that with a bit of work—that is, making the effort to clear the underbrush—I couldn't better develop some of the skills on the other side of my brain that might help bring me into a place of deeper relationship with God.

It takes *all* of our selves. *All* of our everything. *All* of the things we know and *all* of the things we have yet to discover. That means doing the work to create new pathways in our brains.

In order to do that, I have begun watching how kiddos approach various problems and situations. Everything is new to them. They naturally try to figure out how to solve a problem and generally have no clue which part of their brain they are engaging in the process . . . they just go at it until it is solved.

Like many junior high girls, I babysat friends' and neighbors' kids to earn a little extra money. My mom was my best marketing tool for my babysitting business because if she saw someone pushing a stroller in our neighborhood, she would find a way to ask if they needed a reliable babysitter. Thanks to her, I was booked most weekends and also many weekdays during the summer.

When I look back, I realize I learned a lot of really useful things during my babysitting career. I learned that even if you are watching them closely, you could miss a child pushing four green peas up their nose. I learned that bubbles are a great distraction for a baby that doesn't want his Mom to leave without him. And I learned that you will find a better solution to a problem when you approach it from different directions.

I know . . . one of these things is not like the others!

One of my favorite families to babysit for were the McDowells. They moved into a house on the other end of our block. I began babysitting for them when they had one little girl who was two years old named Kelly—and her little baby brother was about to arrive at any moment. The first time I was scheduled to babysit for them, I arrived a little early to get familiar with their home and their preferences. Kelly's Mom walked me through where everything was, how to contact them in case of emergency and all of those other necessary things for taking care of their daughter.

We had almost finished going over the checklist when Kelly and her Dad, Josh, walked in from the backyard—it was my chance to meet her for the first time. She was the cutest thing! She had a sprinkling of freckles across her nose, a twinkle of mischief in her eyes and a smile that would melt your heart . . . I just knew we were going to have a good time together.

Before her parent's left for their evening out, Josh got down on one knee to give her a hug and some last minute admonishments.

> *"Kelly, your Mom and I love you and want you to have a good time with Jann while we are gone."*
>
> Kelly was keenly inquisitive. " *I love you too Daddy! Can she read to me?"*
>
> *"Of course she can—she likes books too!"*
>
> Kelly's little forehead wrinkled. *"How do you know that she likes books?"*
>
> *"Well, we can ask her—that's a good way to find out if she likes books or not."*
>
> *"What if she doesn't?"* The question was obviously very important.
>
> Josh chimed back in, *"Let's ask her before we worry about if she does or doesn't like books."*
>
> *Ok, that sounds like a good idea . . . but I am going to be really sad if she doesn't like books. [Without taking a breath, she continued.] "Dad, if she doesn't like books, would you ask her if she likes to color? Sometimes people who don't like books are still good colorers."*
>
> Josh smiled and replied, *"You're right and that is exactly what we should do!"*

This whole exchange happened eyeball to eyeball and in the most somber of tones. Kelly wasn't being sassy—she was trying her best to be a problem solver and I appreciated the way her Dad didn't try to hurry through the conversation so he and her Mom could get out the door. He stayed present with her in the moment and let her process.

To finish the story, Josh encouraged Kelly to ask me herself if I liked to read books. I assured her that I really did love to read books and then she fired back with a follow-up question, "How do you feel about coloring?"

I almost exploded into laughter because it felt like I was having a conversation with a little adult—but I didn't dare giggle because she was so earnestly focused and I sensed that she would be hurt if I were to fail to consider her question with the same seriousness in which she had asked it. I promised that we would do *both* coloring and reading before it was time for bed.

Problem solved!

Even at her young age, Kelly had already instinctively discovered that the first response doesn't always answer the whole question . . . and her Dad encouraged her to keep asking questions until she got a complete answer that satisfied her curiosity.

Now that is a great pathway to have in your hip pocket! It will probably not surprise you to know that Kelly grew up to be a medical doctor who has a heart for missions and ministry. She is a remarkable young woman and I'm convinced that much of this is due in part to the way her parents encouraged her to process information when she had a problem she needed to solve.

One of my favorite things about *Illuminated Journaling* is that it encourages me to approach my relationship with God from as many pathways as possible. Some are comfortable and well worn—like when I focus on word studies or look for other passages of Scripture that deal with the same theme or topic.

Others are less comfortable, but are becoming more well worn every day—like when I write a poem or prayer in response to my studies or I choose to forget that I can't draw and illustrate my response to God with a bit of art.

Don't get me wrong. My first attempts were pretty pitiful. I wanted to give up. But even when the resulting art wasn't beautiful, the insight I gained into the heart of God while doing it was all the reward I needed to attempt it again.

And, again.—and, again.

And if you could get a bird's eye view of my brain and compare it to the same view when I started, you would see all kinds of new pathways leading to some of the most breathtaking moments I have ever experienced in my walk with the Lord.

There is a certain freshness to it that only comes from stepping off the well-worn trail to follow His voice as it beckons us to search for Him off of the beaten path. When we do so, we are following Jesus' command to love God with *all of our heart, all of our soul and all of our mind.*

Yes, Jesus certainly knew what it would take for us to be in right relationship with Him. It takes *all* of our selves. *All* of our everything—even the parts we don't yet know are there.

Illumination

I was blessed to be adopted as an older child into a family that loved Jesus. His presence in my life became just as normal and expected as Saturday morning pancakes, trips to my grandparents' house and prayer over family dinner. Even so, I've always still been able to remember my life *before*.

Before I had a Mom and a Dad. *Before* someone was there to tuck me into bed at night. *Before* I "belonged" to a family. *Before* I had a precious sister. *Before* . . . when there were scary things that went bump in the night and no one was there to protect me from them. *Before* . . . when being an older child meant you probably wouldn't ever have a family because people wanted babies.

That was *before*.

But *after*!

That's the story I love to tell! *After* I was adopted, I had a family that engulfed me in love. They taught me to love Jesus and His Word. I had a future and a hope—both here on earth

and eternally. And I was an *heir*! It is perhaps one of the very best-est things about being adopted. An adopted child knows what it means to have the course of their life changed when *they become part of a family*. An heir has an inheritance . . . perhaps not a financial inheritance, but an inheritance of belonging—an inheritance of being a part of something bigger than yourself. And if you were not born into a family, you learn what it means for a family to choose to make you part of their family . . . their heir.

That's what Jesus did for *each* of us when He saved us through His death on the cross. Titus says[21], "*He saved us, not because of works done by us in righteousness, but according to His own mercy, by the washing of regeneration and renewal of the Holy Spirit, whom He poured out on us richly through Jesus Christ our Savior, so that being Justified by His grace we might become heirs according to the hope of eternal life.*"

That set me on a life long journey to know my Heavenly Father, Jesus my Savior and the Holy Spirit my Comforter. I studied the Word. I prayed. I've read countless books and listened to pastors and speakers share what they know about them. I was curious and intentional about satisfying that curiosity. I became discontent to walk the same old pathways in my search for Him.

But, to be totally transparent, there have been times when that curiosity waned. I remained in love with them, but I got distracted by life. I got distracted by ministry. I got distracted by sin. I got distracted by thinking I could rely on all the work I put into getting to know them in past years. I began to take only the familiar paths . . . and slowly became unaware that there was so much more.

For me, *Illuminated Journaling* has brought me back to that feeling of "awe" that I am a child of God . . . *His* heir. As I have spent time not just studying, but tarrying in the Word as I seek to meet with Him on the pages of my Bible, I have learned so much more about my inheritance. Some days it is the refreshing of an idea I have known for years; but on others, I learn something so *new* about Him that I can't help but find a way to capture it in a tangible way in my Journaling Bible.

And one of my favorite things that Bible Journaling has brought to my walk with the Lord is this: the art and the words I have placed onto the pages of my Bible have the ability to instantly bring back to my present memory the impact they had on me when I first learned them. It literally renews my mind. That is part of our inheritance . . . as heirs we have unlimited access to our Father in Heaven and He loves to remind us that He *chose* us! My Journaling Bible has become an interactive love letter from Him to me . . . and also from me to Him!

Before reading this chapter, would you have described yourself as a *left-brained* or a *right-brained* person? What things do you do or skills do you have that fall outside of that description?

Describe one or two of the well-worn paths you use to approach God in His Word?

God doesn't want you to limit yourself to just these pathways. He has given you so much more. Paul opens his first letter to the Corinthians with these words[22], *"I give thanks to my God always for you because of the grace of God that was given you in Christ Jesus, that in every way you were enriched in him in all speech and all knowledge—*  *even as the testimony about Christ was confirmed among you—so that you are not lacking in any gift, as you wait for the revealing of our Lord Jesus Christ."*

Did you hear that? You, dear one are " . . . not lacking in *any* gift!" If you were to start with the thing you described as being an ability of yours that falls outside the accepted left or right-brained descriptions, what is one way you could incorporate that gift or skill into your Bible Study time?

And now—a potentially scary question. If you were to try one way to improve your relationship with your Heavenly Father that you would consider *way* outside your comfort zone, what would it be?

Click Stop

It's time to forge ahead with creating a new path. Get your machete and follow me!

Turn back to Matthew 22:37 and, use one of the Margin Templates in the Resource section or a separate journal to break through some of the underbrush and express to God your desire to love Him will all of your heart, soul and mind!

It doesn't have to be an illustration, but it can be. Just let it be an offering from your gifts that may not be so well exercised.

CHAPTER FOUR

An Invitation To Tarry

Confession time. I am not a good waiter. *At. All.*

I don't like waiting in traffic. I will drive a longer distance to be able to keep moving.

I don't like waiting in a doctor's office. I will pick up a six-year-old issue of *Highlights* children's magazine and search for the hidden objects—again—until the nurse calls my name.

I don't like waiting on an answer. As a child, I was tempted to not even ask the question if I didn't think I would get an immediate response.

I don't like waiting. Period. *At. All.*

Ah, but *tarrying* is a different thing altogether. It is an old fashioned word you don't hear very much anymore. It means, "to linger."

Tarrying is not like waiting. *At. All.*

When you tarry, it is   because you want to stay where you are for just another moment or two. Like on those summer evenings when you were a child and your Mom would call

you to come inside just as the first fireflies were beginning to appear, it was almost painful to tear yourself away from the sparkling goodness and go back inside. You were convinced (and you were right) that there was magic happening in the night air and you just couldn't bear to miss out on it.

Tarrying holds promise and must be savored. *Illuminated Journaling* delivers an invitation for you to tarry in God's Word. And it isn't one of those chintzy little postcard invitations. No, your invitation to tarry in the Word comes with a creamy outer envelope that holds the crisp inner envelope with your name written in black calligraphy. When you open it, you will find the printed invitation covered with a sheer piece of vellum. Behind the invitation is your RSVP card. This is the invitation of a lifetime and you will not want to miss it!

Are you at all intrigued? I hope so.

So you are probably wondering, *"What does tarrying look like when I accept the invitation and show up to this party?"*

The process of *tarrying in the Word* is a Bible study method that closes the loop in a repeatable cycle of

Reading → Reflecting → Responding.

We often leave out the response portion of this cycle. We study and reflect, but it often stops there. One of the best things about *Illuminated Journaling* is that it provides a way of responding to God's Word in the exact spot where the lesson was learned. It becomes a tool in my study toolbox. And my tool may look a little different than yours because tarrying is personal.

Here is what tarrying is not. I rarely begin working in my *Illuminated Journaling* Bible immediately after I have completed a study. There are certainly exceptions, but for the most part, to begin immediately would feel like I was forcing myself to describe an experience that I had not yet fully savored. I'm not very knowledgeable about winemaking—but I remember an old commercial on television with the tag line: *"We will sell no wine before its time!"* I thought it was a brilliant commercial at the time because it communicated to the consumer that the quality of their experience was worth the time it took to make it right.

That is how I feel about the response process in *Illuminated Journaling*. Rarely is my first thought my best thought. My goal is not to figure out how to create a journaling page in my Bible as quickly as possible. I prefer to linger . . . to tarry and see what other things occur to me.

Most of the time, this process takes place over a few hours or a few days. But sometimes, it takes weeks or months. I think about it when I am driving (the long way to keep moving.) I think about it when I am cooking or grocery shopping. I talk to God about it during my prayer times. During these times—tarrying is really just an extension of the reflection part of the cycle. Where it begins to differentiate itself is as I begin to "try on" ideas of imagery that I may want to use when I journal about it.

It is a lot like going into the dressing room with a stack of dresses to try on. You've kind of pre-selected a few options before you enter. But once it is just you and that poorly lit room with the wavy mirror, your decision-making begins in earnest. Because, while all of the dresses are nice, they may not be perfect for you and that is exactly the reason why you must try them on before you decide.

Here are a few things I do to decide if an illustration is a good fit for me.

Identify what about this study grabbed my heart and mind. This isn't always a new thought or idea, but it is the one that if someone said it out loud in your hearing, your heart would want to respond with an affirming, *"Mmmm hmmmm, that's right!"* Your head might even start nodding involuntarily—it resonates with you that much.

Hebrews describes the Word of God this way. *"For the word of God is living and active, sharper than any two-edged sword, piercing to the division of soul and of spirit, of joints and of marrow, and discerning the thoughts and intentions of the heart."* If I try on an illustration and it seems to dull the edge of the sword, I know I haven't found the right one yet.

One cautionary suggestion I offer you at this stage of tarrying is: *don't throw out a perfectly good idea because you don't think you could draw it. Mmmm hmmm.* Ask me how I know you need to avoid that!

We are going to talk more about this in Chapters 5 and 8, but let me just assure you right now that God is not going to have a hard time discerning what it is you have added to your page if you first study, reflect and then ask Him His opinion on what needs to go on your page.

Beyond the two of you, no one else should get a say in the matter. I will certainly give you some tips and tricks in later chapters to assist you in adding illustrations to your Bible, even if you don't feel that you can draw, but the bottom line is this: try on several ideas and stick with the one that looks best on *you*.

Think about if the thing I am trying to express is a simple or a complex idea. This may seem like an idea that came straight from *Captain Obvious*, but let me explain. Even a simple idea or thought may actually be made up of several different elements. My entry for Philippians 3:13 called *Yesterday Ended Last Night* that I shared with you in Chapter 2 revolves around a very simple idea, but is made up of several layers that are very personal to me. The sunrise on the new day over the mountains gives visual reference to other scriptures I instantly think of when I see this page. This page represents a simple idea, but the best illustration was more complex.

Likewise, I have found that complex concepts sometimes are best represented by iconic imagery. If I am journaling about the ways Christ has changed the very fiber of my being, a butterfly emerging from a cocoon might be the perfect image to add to that page.

Right now, I have two differ- ent journal entries that I am in the middle of working on simul- taneously. In my mind, they come as a pair. The first is: *Pray for Israel*. The second *is: Pray for the United States*. My journal entry, *Pray for Israel*, finally felt right when I landed on an image of a   Jewish man covered in a prayer shawl standing at the Western Wall in Jerusalem[23].

The image is iconic and embodies the complex thoughts of what I am praying for when I say *Pray for Israel.* Zechariah reminds us *"He who touches [Israel] touches the apple of His eye."* I pray for them to no longer wail in frustration that their Messiah has not yet come. I want them to know Jesus. I want to support them in the battle against the enemies that desire to destroy them and wipe them from the face of the earth. The Western Wall is important to all who would call Jerusalem their home, and this image says more than I could ever explain in the small space of this page.

I tried on many images in my mind, yet I knew when I saw this one that I had found my inspiration photo. At the printing of this book, I have not yet found my inspiration photo for *Pray for the United States*, but I will continue to go through this process until I find an image that sits well in my soul—and then I will begin to make it work on the pages of my Bible.

Which reminds me to share this thought: part of what makes tarrying in the Word so sweet is that there is no pressure to get the journal entry made *today.* If you don't feel that you've found the right fit, put a place holder on the page to remind yourself that the page is "spoken for" and then continue with the process of thinking and trying on ideas until you find the one that will do what you want it to do.

When I feel that I have settled on at least a direction for my page, *I begin to think through the elements I want to include.* This usually doesn't take a long time, but creating a mental list of how much room I will need to reserve for each element will help me with some of my other design decisions. This is also when I check to see what kind of space I have available to work with in my Bible. Since I do not study out of this Bible, I don't always know what the page looks like. Are the margins on the page with my chosen verse on the left or right? Has something already been journaled about on the page? Do the verses happen to fall where there is more open space like at the end of a book?

All of these things need to be taken into consideration when you begin to design your entry. Once I have seen the page and the area I will be working in, I can begin to contemplate how I will adapt my plan for the space allowed.

Some of the elements you may want to consider at this stage in your plan are: *titles, quotes, imagery* and *journaling.* You don't have to have all of these elements on every page. Some will only contain one or two, but it is helpful if you begin to plan out how much space you need to keep for each of the elements you want to include.

This becomes even more important if you have chosen to confine your design to the margins only. I have found this is a good time to grab a sketchpad and give your idea a rough sketch . . . no need to make it precise.

I am a visual processor and seeing it in rough form allows me to evaluate if it feels crowded or if the elements are balanced and proportional. I have even sometimes written out my journaling during this time—not on the page itself, but maybe beside my sketch. Journaling is so important and I find that if I don't plan and keep enough space for it, I end up squeezing it in—or trying to edit it down to the space allowed.

One place to add journaling without eating up the whole page is by using a *tip in* [an addition to a page that looks a bit like a flap]. *Tip ins* are a great way to gain some extra real estate on your page. They can be made from so many different things. I have used parts of a bulletin, a piece of watercolor paper, a hotel key card, a coaster from a restaurant, a tag or a piece of printed artwork. *Tip ins* are added to the page with some form of adhesive. I like using

washi tape because it is decorative, thin and acts as a hinge. If I need room for private journaling, or I want to add a piece of paper that contains an important element of my design, I build my design plan around it as a *tip in*[24]. The other benefit of a *tip in* is that you can use part of it as the place to put your title or main thought. You can be as creative as you like once you determine that you will be adding an additional element onto your page.

You may be thinking that these things I have just shared make sense for the style of *Illuminated Journaling* that *I* do, but adding images into your Bible isn't your style and you are not sure how to apply this process to a hand lettering or modern collage style.

I think the process can still be applied when you apply it to making decisions about where you want the viewer to focus. Here are a couple of examples of hand lettering that I have

done. Jeremiah 29:11[25] is jam packed with power and I didn't feel that I wanted anything other than the words to be the focus. But even then, there were so many options that I felt I needed to narrow it down. So I tarried with it a while. I doodled on some scratch paper to see how I could emphasize the particular words that I had focused on in my study. I certainly could have gone many directions and it would have been good, but I finally settled on wanting to emphasize the words "plans," "You," "Lord," "Hope" and "Future." As I did the hand lettering, I only added color to those five words so they would stand out on the page.

My entry entitled, *I Need Christ*[26], is another example of how I applied the tarrying principle to a page that does not

contain an image. This entry is a quote by C.S. Lewis and makes no direct reference to a passage of scripture. I could have chosen to place it on one of the reference pages at the back of my Bible—but after tarrying a while, I felt like this bold statement was a great way to introduce the whole book of Philippians.

I matched the boldness of the statement with bright colors that stood out against the backdrop of blues and greens. Your lettering or collage *is* the imagery that you have chosen to use. When you tarry and ponder how best to make the lettering communicate, your choices of color, focus, size, and style create an impression along with the words.

Finally, it may seem that it should go without saying, but *I ask the Lord for His opinion* as I consider what I might do. Of the two of us, He is much more creative than I am—and I have found that just talking about it with Him usually brings a new thought or idea to my mind. This isn't a formal process by any means. It is much more of an open-ended discussion, but it almost always helps me to get unstuck. I often apply the promise of James 1:5 to this situation—*"If any of you lacks wisdom, let him ask God who gives generously without reproach and it will be given to him."* God loves to help us out when we are stuck . . . so be sure and invite Him into the process. I know you will love the results!

So now you know—I don't just sit down and draw in my Bible. I do enjoy the creation process very much when I get to the point where I am ready to close the ***Read→ Reflect→ Respond*** cycle. It is fun and I have actually begun to think of it as a way to give an offering of praise and thanksgiving back to God for all that I have learned as I prepared to make this entry. It is kind of a "first-fruits" offering. I have reaped so much benefit from studying the Word in this manner . . . it has changed my life and my relationship with God. The Bible instructs us that when we reap a harvest, we ought to give a "first-fruits" offering as a sacrifice of praise[27]. This is one way I can do that. I find that when I revisit the page later, I also remember the benefits that God added to my storehouse while I was working on it . . . blessing upon blessing!

You can't out give God!

After learning to appreciate the process of tarrying in the Word, I now compare it to making a good beef stew. (I told you I don't know much about wine making, but I *am* an expert beef stew chef.) If you want a really good beef stew, you don't need expensive ingredients. Good stew can be made from cheap cuts of beef, root vegetables and some seasoning. The key to making it great is time. You can't rush beef stew . . . you have to cook it low and slow. And even when it's done, it's better the next day [especially if you add a splash of V8 juice].

Time. Your journaling will always benefit from you giving it time. Tarry and let the seasoning of the Spirit work His way down into your soul. It's kind of magical . . . like fireflies on a summer evening!

Illumination

Make sure you have your Bible near by. Consider a passage of Scripture you have come in contact with recently that has captured your heart or your mind. It could be something shared during a sermon, a devotional or conversation with a friend. Turn to that passage and use it to fill in these questions.

Read: What is the passage? Write the reference. If you have room, write out the passage here on the page.

Reflect: What about this passage has captivated you? As you have reflected on it's meaning in your life, write a few sentences that explain the context and its significance, along with any new insight you have gained as you have reflected upon it.

Respond: Is there a call to action? Does it inspire you to change something in your life—or implement its command or instruction? If so, what is your response to that command or instruction? If it is a promise, what does that promise mean in your life? (You may need to think about this a bit . . . tarrying takes . . . time!)

Click Stop

How could you portray what you have learned from this passage? List three ideas of imagery that you might "try on" to see how they fit.

1._____

2._____

3._____

What are two titles you might use?

1._____

2._____

Sometimes journaling helps us "tie up" loose ends, giving us a place to write what we intend to do with this new knowledge, or adding context that is significant. Write your journaling about this passage here.

Draw a sketch of your idea here or on one of the Margin Templates in the Resource Section, and if you are comfortable with it, go ahead and add it to your Journaling Bible.

CHAPTER FIVE

You Do Have A Creative
Bone In Your Body

"So what do those of us do that don't have a creative bone in our body?"

I was so startled by her question that I blurted out, *"You stop underestimating your skeleton!"*

I still laugh when I think about that first workshop I taught on the subject of *Illuminated Journaling*. I had been asked to speak at a women's retreat and the Women's Ministry Director had asked me specifically to share about *Illuminated Journaling*, even though she didn't think anyone attending had ever heard of such a thing. I was excited to get to share something I had become passionate about, but I was also a tad bit nervous.

Now you have to understand, I am rarely nervous in situations like this . . . I love teaching. I love teaching from the Word even more, add the opportunity to teach a group of women from the Word about *Illuminated Journaling* and I am living just this side of heaven!

My nervousness came from the initial response of some people to the pages from my Bible that I had shared on my blog. Most were very encouraging. However, a few, like my friend's email I shared in chapter one, needed some reassurance that I was not bringing the fires of hell down on my head. Then there were some who were frankly appalled and felt it was their duty to actually call down the fires of hell upon my head just in case the Holy Spirit had missed what I was up to.

I wasn't sure where this group of women was going to land and I wanted to be prepared. I was so expecting the very first question to be about the theology of drawing in my Bible that I was utterly unprepared for her question about creativity—thus I blurted out the first thing that came to me, *"You stop underestimating your skeleton!"*

What I said to her, I say to you in slightly different terms. You do have a creative bone in your body, even if you aren't sure where to find it. We are all made in the image of God—and He is the Creator! As imperfect as we are, each of us has within us some seed of creativity because we are made like Him.

I know few of us will ever paint something worthy of being hung in the Louvre, but creativity surfaces in many forms. We naturally think of creativity in association with some sort of art-oriented hobby, but creativity is really all about stewarding our gifts and talents by applying them to the task at hand, whatever it may be.

One of my mentors used to say that being creative is not something you are or you are not, rather it is something you tap into. And if you are one of those who have a harder time finding the mouth of the well that leads down into your own personal creativity, this chapter will help you "dig a little deeper" and tap into your God given reservoir.

My Dad used to tell me that he had never seen anyone do math problems with such creative flare . . . and he didn't mean it as a compliment! I was not great at math. When working on word problems, I was much more interested in *who was taking the train leaving at noon* than how fast they were traveling or at what time they would pass the other train that left at 2:00 pm.

Why would we need to know what time they passed each other? Was someone on the other train going to toss a package to the person on this train that would save the world from certain destruction? Now *that's* interesting! But ask me to figure out the correct formula and I would end up with all of my x's, y's and z's in a jumble. So I struggled on.—feeling inept and discouraged.

Then in eighth grade, I had a math teacher who seemed to teach math in a different way—well, at least it was new to me and it made sense. He found a way to help me understand the importance of defining variables and coefficients [did a shiver just go down your spine, too?] And while I am never going to take home the top prize in a math competition, I no longer think I have zero ability to do anything vaguely associated with math. My ability was always there, but it took a teacher who knew where to look for it to help me find it.

If you are in search of your creative bone—or you just want to ramp up your access to it—the rest of this chapter is going to focus on five practical things you can do to tap in to your God given creativity and maximize it in all areas of your life, not just *Illuminated Journaling*.

One| Feed Your Curiosity

Curiosity may have killed the cat—but not feeding your creativity with curiosity will certainly stifle your ability to access your creativity.

Has anyone ever offered to share some sour dough starter or friendship bread with you? If not, then if someone ever does make that offer, run as fast as you can the other way! You will become slave to the bread!

Well, maybe I am exaggerating, but only a little. Friendship bread requires that you feed the dough in your refrigerator at regular intervals, bake some bread from it and then share a portion with a friend. I like baking bread, so of course I said yes when my friend offered some to me.

But that bread became a hungry monster! I felt like my whole life schedule began to revolve around if it were time to feed the dough, bake the dough or share the dough—and it only got worse when another friend shared some of hers with me as well. I didn't have the heart to tell her that I was already *dough-nuts*! That's what my family began to call the crazy look in my eye when I had to go into the kitchen to take care of the dough.

No, this is not a book on avoiding crazy kitchen trends. My point in bringing it up is to reinforce the fact that you *have* to feed your curiosity if you want it to develop into something useful. Give your brain something to think about.

Everything you put into your Bible doesn't have to be an original thought. Go and see what other Journalers are posting on *Instagram* or *Pinterest*. Be inspired by what you see and then take the next step, thinking about how you would adapt it if you were to do something similar. That is creative exercise at it's best.

I also feed my creativity when I allow myself to *tarry in the Word*. As I have mentioned before, I rarely finish a study session and move directly into documenting it in my Journaling Bible. I let it set for a bit. When I am doing other chores, I think about how I would illustrate the main points. I try out lots of ideas in my head long before I sit down and add them to my Bible. By feeding my creativity with possible ideas and letting them wander around in my head for a few days, I may discover something really terrific that would never have occurred to me if I had moved immediately into adding the illustration into my Bible.

Two| Collect Ideas

I am a collector of ideas. Sometimes I have so many ideas that I feel like I am a sponge so full of water that I am leaking around the edges. If I want my collection to be helpful, it also has to be organized.

That is why I really love *Pinterest™*. Yes, I know it can be a "time sucker" and you have to be careful to not spend more time looking for creative ideas than actually creating. But the thing I think it does really well is to provide a fresh batch of ideas every time you log in—*and* it provides a handy way to organize the ideas that you want to save for future reference.

If you have never checked it out or if you have wisely stayed away until you had a specific need for it, I would suggest that you at least go to Pinterest.com and take a look around. In the Resource section at the back of the book, I have provided a list of search words you can use to get you started. I highly recommend setting up a couple of your own Pinterest Boards . . . think of it like a personal bulletin board where you can post lists, pictures or other ideas so they are accessible later. If you visit my Pinterest Boards, you will see that I use them to keep a wide collection of ideas organized and accessible when I need them. My two boards you may find the most helpful (link in Resource section) would be *Illuminated Journaling* and *Faith.*—but you might also enjoy my *Color Inspiration* and *Cool Typography* boards too.

The other way I collect ideas is in several physical file folders that I keep near my desk. I throw pages from magazines, junk mail with interesting images, paint swatches from the hardware store, pieces of paper with words on them in innovative text treatments and anything else that catches my eye into those folders so I can just flip through them when I need some inspiration.

Collecting ideas gives you a place to start when you need some inspiration and will provide you with an "x marks the spot" location to start digging to tap into your own creative well.

Three| Use The Tools Available To You as Creatively As You Can

When I first started journaling in my Bible, I could only think of two ways to add "art" into it: I could trace it or I could stamp it—and both of those felt like cheating. In my head, I was thinking, "A real artist would be able to just sit down and draw something into their Bible." But I did it anyway . . . because it was the only way I knew how.

Then one day I was talking with a dear friend who is a missionary and was trying to put together a special event with very little access to the supplies she needed. I said, "Use what you have, God will provide you with ways to creatively use them beyond their apparent capacity." As soon as I said the words, they suddenly felt like they were for me as much as her. Has God ever done that to you? You're in the middle of providing advice to someone else and He smacks you on the head with a "wow, I could have had a V8" kind of moment? Okay, maybe it is just me . . . but I clearly got the message.

I had been giving less than my best to my journaling because I thought I had been cheating instead of trying to find ways to use what I had to create the best offering on the pages of my Bible. When I dropped the "stinkin' thinkin'" about tracing and stamping and saw them as ways to begin accessing my creativity for my journal entries, I saw dramatic changes in the results. I was so focused on what I *couldn't* do that I was missing out on taking what I had and making it incredible.

I now teach a whole six-lesson workshop on "The Art of Tracing[28]." There are so many other ways to express your creativity in your composition once you have the basic shape added to your page that two people who have traced the same elements onto the same page of their respective Bibles will always create two very different results because each has found a way to express their own creativity. I've moved beyond thinking that the only creativity that counts is that which I create completely from scratch . . . and I want to encourage you to begin thinking that way as well. See if it doesn't have an impact on how you view your creativity, as well as the results you achieve.

Four| Experiment and Practice

When I need a bit of a jumpstart for my creativity, I set aside some time to do what I like to call *Creative Play*. I go into my studio and pull out just a few of my tools, products or supplies—and I just have fun. I don't work in my Bible when I am having a creative play session—my whole purpose is to experiment and see what I am capable of doing with those supplies I have brought to my desk.

If you are like me, I sometimes see something that another Journaler has done and when I look to see what supplies she used to create it, I find out she has listed a product I have never even thought of using before . . . and then I want to try it out. So I put it on my wish list and when finances allow, I pick it up and wait for an opportunity to try it out. *Creative Play* is an excellent time to pull out the new product to see what it is capable of, while familiarizing yourself with its properties.

The other benefit of *Creative Play* time is that you may discover a new use for a supply you already have. Figuring out what your products are capable of doing and how they interact with each other when you are not in the middle of working on a page can be a great source of inspiration when you begin working on a journal entry.

You will be bolder in your use of your products and supplies if you are confident that you know what results you are likely to achieve with them. So take time to experiment and then be intentional about using what you learn in your journaling.

Practice. Why does it feel like I just wrote a four-letter word? To me, this word conjures up old mental images of playing piano scales for hours on end while my bike was beckoning me to jump on and ride. That was practice. But in reality, such images shouldn't dominate my thoughts. Anything that we want to do well requires practice.

Creativity requires practice. Creativity is like a muscle that will atrophy if you don't use it. Practice doesn't have to be boring. Just like I use *Creative Play* to experiment with my products and tools, I use *Creative Practice* to hone my skills.

One of the skills I have been very intentional about practicing is hand lettering. I love what I see other Journalers do in their Bibles by using creative lettering to emphasize some words or add a creative twist to a phrase or thought. I don't have bad handwriting, but it needed some sprucing up to make it capable of expressing what I wanted it to on my pages. I carry a graph paper tablet with me in my purse. If I find myself with a few minutes on my hands, I pull out my graph paper and practice. I print off a page of letters in different font styles and just practice them on my graph paper until I can reproduce them with ease. By practicing, I add a new skill to my toolbox and that skill affords me more creative options to use when I begin working in my Bible.

Five| Seek Out Kindred And Not So Kindred Spirits

I am an *Anne of Green Gables* fan. I try to find time every couple of years to reread the whole series from start to finish . . . it just reminds me of what having a positive and encouraging spirit can accomplish. I must confess that in my younger days, I would look in the mirror and wish that I had glorious red hair to pile up on my head like Anne. But alas, it was not meant to be.

One of my favorite quotes is when she sighs contentedly to Marilla (her adopted Mom,) *"Kindred Spirits are not so scarce as I used to think. It's splendid to find out that there are so many of them in the world.*[29]*"* If I had begun *Illuminated Journaling* several years ago, it would have been a solitary proposition. I still would have been blessed in my relationship with the Lord, but I wouldn't have had the access to all of the *kindred spirits* who are also pursuing a closer relationship with God by journaling in their Bibles too. Social media has made it possible for us to find others who are our *kindred spirits* and have interactions with them in ways that were never possible before.

If you have stumbled upon *Illuminated Journaling* without learning about it via social media, you are in for a treat. Go check out Instagram and Pinterest for loads of inspiration and look into finding a Facebook Group to participate in. I have listed several of them for you in the Resource section of this book. Some are considered closed groups, just to help keep them safe environments for everyone participating. You can request to join and an administrator will give you access. Be sure and read the information each of them provides when you first join. Most have very few rules, but you will want to familiarize yourself with them before you jump into posting or commenting.

I have found people in the Facebook Groups to provide me with some of the best creative inspiration I've ever received—sometimes because they are obviously *kindred spirits,* but sometimes because they obviously are not. These groups are comprised of about as diverse a group of Christians as you would ever hope to meet. Theology, perspectives and preferences are wide and varied. Yet most of the time, we manage to set those aside and just focus on the Lord—and there is always something to spark my creativity when the focus is on Him! I believe there will be for you as well.

Creativity is not just found in crème of the crop artists, designers, dancers, singers, writers, doodlers, and illustrators. Creativity is in *you* . . . placed there by God along with His desire for you to use it. You are the only one who can present a sacrificial offering of your creativity back to Him. Don't miss out on that opportunity.

Illumination

Doing What Scares You

I bet you almost quit reading.

I'm not judging . . . I almost quit writing!

Fear is a two-sided coin. It keeps us from stepping off the curb without looking both ways. It keeps us from opening our door to a stranger. It keeps us safe—and that is a good thing.

But fear can also paralyze us. If we are afraid of *failing*, it can keep us from trying new things because we won't do them *perfectly*—and anything *less than* perfect is unacceptable. I think we all struggle with this brand of fear in one way or another.

Oh, I have met people who appear to be *fearless* when it comes to trying new things, but what I have found is that they are not *fear*-less—they are *brave*-ful. Yes, I know I just made up a word . . . but it worked better than saying they are super duper brave.

This truth applies to so many aspects of our lives, but let's narrow the focus to journaling in our Bibles. How can we become *brave*-ful in our *Illuminated Journaling*?

Here are three tips to help all of us on the road to being *brave*-ful.

1. **Schedule some fear-bopping *"try it* time**." My grandmother had a single phrase she used when she heard me say that I didn't think I could do something.

"You'll never know until you try!" You see, I haven't always been *brave*-ful. I came into this world with an exaggerated fondness for perfection—and clearly some misguided thinking that people who were "good" at certain things probably did them well the first time they tried. My grandmother's phrase was her attempt to motivate me to at least go and make a valiant attempt.

Fortunately, she won that battle with me often enough that I now have that conversation in my head the minute I start thinking, *"I couldn't do that."*

My tip for chasing away the *"I couldn't"* thought is to schedule a time to try it. Maybe not in your Bible,

but definitely sit down and *try it*! Sometimes I use my *Creative Play* time that I described earlier to intentionally attempt a different style. I recently pulled out my acrylic paints and *tried* scraping paint on my page[30] like I have seen so many other journalers do.

Do theirs look better than mine . . . sure they do! But my goal isn't to make my page look like theirs. My goal is to stretch my creative "tool box" and see what I can learn about my *own* style by trying a technique I love seeing someone else use. I wasn't *fear*-less, and maybe I wasn't totally *brave*-ful either . . . but I moved a notch or two in the direction of brave. And that is quite an accomplishment for an hour or so of *Creative Play*.

2. **Go one step further.** When I am painting or drawing, I have added a "finishing touch" technique to my process that I call the *go one step further* technique. If I look at an image that I am "pretty" satisfied with, but not totally wowed by, I try to *go one step further.* For me, that usually means I need to add more lights and darks . . . my image is probably missing *contrast.*

   When I am *fear*-ful, I tend to stop short of doing anything that could potentially ruin what I have been working on—and that means I have usually blended everything together so well that I have lost the highlights and shadows that give the viewers' eyes the clues they need to know that they are actually looking at a 3D object.

   For you, the *go one step further* technique might be adding a drop shadow to your hand lettering or blending your coloring (if you used colored pencils) with some Gamsol or Odorless Mineral spirits. The key is to step outside the comfort zone and take a chance on creating something really *spectacular*! Spectacular doesn't mean perfect. It means that the gift cost you something . . . that you were willing to take a risk.

3. **Do it anyway.** Having shared that I am just a beginner when it comes to hand lettering and that I am still getting less-than-stellar results most of the time doesn't mean I'm waiting until I am perfect to begin hand lettering in my Bible. I'm sure the day will come when I don't see my titles and think, "*Wow, that just didn't turn out how I thought it would in my head.*" But for now, I'm going to keep practicing and keep adding hand lettering into my Journaling Bible. I am going to

remember Who I am creating it for and that my Heavenly Father has already found my gift to Him worthy . . . in part because I'm willing to give Him my imperfections so that He may perfect *me*!

So there you have it. This *Illumination* is not the *Three Easy Steps To Becoming Brave*-ful, but I can honestly say that these have moved me from being *fear*-ful of making a mistake in my Bible to a place of practicing the art of being *brave*-ful when I open my Bible to begin journaling. That is the kind of *fullness* I want to give to God. How about you? To quote my dear Jammy Jane, *"You'll never know until you try!"*

When do you feel you are your most creative self?

What about that experience could you use to help you feel more creative when you are journaling in your Bible?

Which of the three tips that were shared about becoming brave-ful would be the biggest help to you if you were to incorporate one or more of them in your approach to journaling?

What would that look like? Describe how it would change what you do when you sit down to journal.

Click Stop

Read Joshua 1:1-9 and 2 Chronicles 20:15.

Do either of these passages speak to your heart about why God might tell you to *"fear not"* regarding a specific aspect of your life?

Turn back to that passage and either use a Margin Template in the Resource section, the margin of your Bible or a separate journal, dig down deep and use that newly discovered source of creativity to express what you know about His character from the passage. You can draw, trace, stamp, doodle or scribble—the important thing is to be bold in your offering.

CHAPTER SIX

Leaving Your heART
On the Page

"Oh, my hand."

"New parchment, bad ink; I say nothing more."

Writing and drawing in the margins is actually not new at all. Before the printing press, scribes—usually monks—were the copyists of every manuscript, Bible or book. In addition to copying the assigned pages, they couldn't seem to resist leaving behind a few of their own thoughts on the pages as well. Some apparently loved their job and others . . . not so much.

"Thank God it will soon be dark."

"Let the reader's voice honor the writer's pen.[31]"

Marginalia, the proper term for that which is written or drawn into the margins, has intrigued anthropologists and sociologist for years. It is like a window into the soul of the person who took the time to add it to the page. These little additions have seemed to serve multiple purposes from simply entertaining the copyist, to providing a mnemonic device to help the eventual reader retain what they read, to adding to the beauty of the manuscript with illustrations, and, of course, as a commentary or reflection by the scribe.

While you don't find much evidence of marginalia in bound versions of the Bible, we know that it was a common practice among the monks because many unbound pages of partially copied scriptures have an abundance of drawings and thought provoking notes. Copying a page could take days to complete because the scribe had to be very exact. Even the slightest error would render the page unusable.

It seems they would take a break from their work and use the margins to make notes to themselves, try out new pen nibs, create lists of other similar scriptures or ask questions that occurred to them as they spent hours reflecting on the same scripture.

Illuminated manuscripts took even longer. The addition of illustrations or highly stylized letters added value to manuscript, but also increased the likelihood of errors—so it appears that those elements were added first in an attempt to avoid ruining a full page of script should the illuminator's hand waver or a drop of ink fall from the pen onto the paper . . . thus these pages are filled with a treasure trove of marginalia.

If these imperfect pages had been able to be bound into a manuscript, the binding process would have cut off most of the things written in the margin. Of course, I find them fascinating and am so glad that some still exist. I had the opportunity to walk through an exhibit that came to Nashville containing a marvelous collection of Biblical marginalia.

Several things I observed on those centuries old pages have come to influence how I feel about *Illuminated Jour-*

naling today—and it may provide you with some things to ponder as you are deciding how you would like to leave your heART on the pages of your Bible.

As precise as the calligraphy letters of the scripture were, the notes in the margins were done in their own handwriting.

I love adding beautiful hand lettered elements and titles to my pages, but I make a conscious effort to include some of my notes or thoughts in my own handwriting.

My sister and I treasure a Bible that belonged to our grandmother. Jammy Jane (our special name for her) was a godly woman who had an insatiable curiosity about her Heavenly Father and His Word.

She wasn't one to talk much about any subject, but I learned a lot of what the Bible says about being a wife, mother, daughter, friend and Christ follower by watching her live it out every day. She taught fourth and fifth grade girls' Sunday School and her Bible is filled with notes for her lessons, names of the girls printed by scriptures that I believe she used to remind herself to pray for them.

Perhaps my favorite entries are the comments and questions she wrote in the margins. All of her notes, comments and questions, written in her handwriting, provide a tangible bond between her and me that transcends time . . . and these have guided my own walk with the Lord long after she was no longer here for me to learn from.

There are many days I wish I could just call up Jammy Jane and ask for her wisdom and council, and it is on those days I turn to the book that was her source of wisdom and her handwriting points me to the One who knows exactly what I need in that moment.

Handwriting is so personal. It is a way of identifying the writer. I would know my grandmother's handwriting anywhere I saw it—and I want to leave a little bit of myself on the pages of my Bible too. Even if you don't love your handwriting, I would encourage you to find a way to leave a bit of yourself on the pages of your Bible. I sometimes add hidden journaling on the back of a little card that I tape into the page[32]. I believe there is a place for both aesthetically pleasing words and those less perfect, but oh so revealing, lines written in our own handwriting.

Not everything was profound.

The Monks often made note of simple things. They noted the weather or changing of the seasons. They would write a Middle English version of "Yes, Lord!" near to a passage that contained a promise of God. Sometimes the mark was of a dove placed beside a scripture about the Holy Spirit. I love that! It was real and personal.

Most of the things I now add into my *Illuminated Journaling* Bible are not earthshattering. They are important because they are a reflection of the time I have spent with God on the pages of His Word. Sometimes I just feel the need to remind myself of a particular truth. Other times, I simply want to thank Him for the promises I have found there. And still others reflect an ongoing prayer, a captured thought or a moment of simple insight.

Just as my earthly relationships have ebb and flow to them, so does my relationship with God. There are times I approach Him earnestly with a need or request, but most of the time, my entries are about the everyday things that happen between us. When I began journaling in this Illuminated style, I mostly added things that had influenced my relationship with God in some monumental way. And while there is nothing wrong with capturing and memorializing those things, most of my day-to-day interactions with God are not done at a fever pitch.

My days begin with a cup of coffee, reading a passage of scripture, a few moments of reflection and prayer and then I emerge to face the world. I am not a morning person—and God is abundantly aware of that. Our moments together in the morning are more about setting the tone for the day than they are about gaining new knowledge or insight.

Still, those morning meetings are precious to me. If my journaling Bible is going to reflect my relationship with God, then it also needs to reflect those kinds of meetings too. My Bible now has entries that reveal those quiet times, evidence of the reassuring moments when He provided me with the last bit of peace before the storm.

I have come to treasure these simple entries almost as much as those that bring to mind the magnificence of God. I have created my own coding system of little stamps or simple drawings that I use to mark pages with a common theme. They may not be the focus of the page, but as I flip through my Bible, I see just how often I have worked on entries that are about God's love, the Holy Spirit, a promise of God, grace, fear not, finances and family. I'm sure I will develop more over time . . . and I have begun to think about a way to provide the key to the code in the back of my Bible so my family will someday know why they keep seeing a symbol again and again. This is just another way to capture the everyday things that happen when we study God's Word.

They had a sense of humor.

As I walked around the exhibit, I found myself chuckling at some of the drawings. One showed what appears to be a coyote with a duck in its mouth[33]. The doomed duck is letting

out a final *queck*! Okay, so it's not likely that the monk who drew this little cartoon was ever going to get a job drawing pictures for the Sunday comics, but it made me smile when I saw that he had taken the time to write the word "queck" by the duck's beak.

I have kind of a quirky sense of humor and I love to laugh. But in looking through my Bible, I realized that I hadn't let that part of my relationship with God appear on the pages. I probably will never add a post containing knee slapping humor, but I like that now a few of my pages have a touch of my tongue in cheek humor[34] because I certainly have shared a laugh or two with God over the crazy things I have done or thought. He could probably name several more times when He as laughed over the goofy things I have done without even realizing it, but He is too polite to do so right now.

There are also Bible stories that seem to just cry out for a bit of humor in my illustration, even as they provide meaningful lessons. One of my favorites is the story of the irreverent teenage boys and Elisha. The boys from the town began to jeer at him yelling, "Go on, you old bald head!"[35] I've known many a youth pastor that has secretly cheered at what happened next. Two she bears came out of the woods and mauled forty-two of the boys.

The moral of this story is: *respect your elders—especially if you are anywhere near a wooded area where wild animals could come out and devour you. Those animals are smart and will always pass up the old tough skinned youth pastor in favor of your young and easy-to-chew hide.* I am going to keep thinking about this one . . . just know that one day I will figure out exactly how I want to portray it in my Bible.

Don't hesitate to let all of your personality show up on the pages of your Bible. Leave some of your sense of humor there along with your heART.

They didn't have all of the answers.

And neither do I. It would be a poor reflection of who I really am if every entry I made into my Bible was filled with certainty and absolute assurance. God and His Word are true and we can trust both with every fiber of our being, but there are still many things I don't understand . . . and that I may never understand until I stand before Him in His throne room.

Fortunately, God is not put off by my questions or lack of understanding. I'm so glad I have pages in my Bible that reflect my thoughts or feelings prior to being able to see things from God's perspective. These pages provide assurance of His constancy when I see how He has allowed me to wrestle with what I don't understand—only to reveal just how perfectly reasoned and planned His purposes are even when I can't see it. It becomes even a greater joy when I am able to tell the rest of the story, by returning and adding another entry that provides the follow-up.

You may want to consider allowing your journaling to reflect your personal growth or understanding on a topic or passage of scripture. I think of each of my journal entries as a snapshot capturing what I know in that moment. As God reveals Himself and my understanding matures, it is time to take another snapshot. Just like we mark the changing height of our kiddos in the frame of a doorway, these snapshots of our faith will be tangible proof of God's revelation to us as we grow in our walk with Him.

Scriptures prompted prayers, promises and praise.

I have shared with you that I use my *Illuminated Journaling* Bible as a place to respond to God[36]. It is the way I complete the cycle that begins with me *reading* the Word, followed by *reflecting* on what I have read and then finally *responding* to God and the things I have learned. That response often takes the form of written *prayers*, affirming *promises* I have received in the Word, or exclamations of *praise*[37].

I find that being intentional about adding these kinds of pages into my Bible has some terrific benefits. Seeing a prayer reminds me to continue in prayer. Reading a promise reassures me that God is at work on my behalf, even if I have not yet seen the promise completed.

And perhaps most importantly, it allows me to repeat back to God what I have heard Him say. Have you ever been in a conversation with someone and you weren't quite sure they were getting your point? I have been known to ask, "Could you tell me what you heard me say?" Okay, let's be honest, I usually ask that question when I am a bit annoyed and it comes out more like, "*What* did I *just* say!" I think you know which words to emphasize . . . even if you have never uttered them yourself.

At this point in my life, I have too many examples of moments when I totally missed the mark on understanding what God was trying to tell me. It wasn't intentional on my part, but when I haven't given Him a chance to correct me where I am wrong, it has always resulted in trouble down the road.

I have found that the time it takes for me to add a journal entry onto a page is a great time to "tell Him what I heard Him say" and wait to see if I got it right . . . or if He wants me to try again. I know He has no desire for me to   continue in my confusion if I haven't fully understood Him[38] and will use this time to clarify what He really did say.

Because of this, sometimes I end up changing the direction of my post. And that is a good thing. I'm not striving for *perfection* on these pages—I'm striving for *reflection*.

The monks left behind a legacy of God's faithfulness in their lives.

Until recently, most families had a family Bible. It would contain the family records of births, marriages and deaths. It would be passed down from one generation to the next. I can still remember how fascinated I was with our family's Bible when I was a kid—it was the biggest Bible I had ever seen. My grandmother kept it sitting on her coffee table opened to Joshua 24:15, which read, "As for me and my house, we will serve the Lord." It was her unspoken testimony to all who visited her and sat on her couch that our family loved God and had chosen to serve Him.

With the advent of the Internet and the ease of accessing legal documents, the family Bible has become a thing of the past. I believe that your *Illuminated Journaling* Bible, filled with all of your communications with God, will become a treasured heirloom and stand as a testimony to God's faithfulness in the lives of you and your family. If the Lord tarries, you may even have several "Family Bibles" to pass down to future generations. Wouldn't that just be an amazing legacy? I sure think so!

And here is just another crazy idea that I have: I would so love to see churches begin to provide a Journaling Bible to the parents of each child at their dedication instead of the small white Bibles that are often given now. How cool would it be for the family to begin filling that child's Bible with prayers, letters and other notes of encouragement or praise beginning from their birth and continuing until it is presented to them as they make preparations to leave home and begin the next chapter in their lives.

Their Bible would contain a personalized testimony of God's faithfulness, love and provision in their lives up to that point and a reminder of the legacy of faith that is the firmest of foundations upon which they can build their future.

Now *that's* a family Bible!

Whether you have a family filled with cousins twice removed (but they keep coming back) or you are a family of one, this family Bible is about your heavenly family as much as your earthly one. Keep a record of all the significant happenings and be sure and leave a bit of your heART on the page.

Illumination

"The grass withers, the flower fades, but the Word of our God endures forever!"
-- Isaiah 40:8

Forever! I think this verse is one of the main reasons I feel so strongly about this journey that you have embarked upon. The time you put into studying the Word, meditating on it and reflecting on His teachings as you create your own marginalia is time spent on something of immeasurable worth. God's Word is indestructible.

Every moment we spend hiding His Word in our hearts is infinitely valuable. It somehow seemed right to put the prettiest flowers I could around these words[39] . . . because even as beautiful as they are . . . they will fade.

Nothing compares to the eternal beauty of God's Holy Word.

Here is a condensed list of the various uses of marginalia. If you can, make a brief note of a verse, story or illustration you would consider adding to your journaling Bible.

Handwritten Entry

Simple Insight

Humor

Questions You May Have

Prayers

Promises

Praises

Legacy of Faith

Click Stop

As you wrote examples or ideas of how you might use marginalia, which are you most anxious to make part of your *Illuminated Journaling* Bible?

What about it appeals to you?

Ask God how He would like you to leave your heART on the pages of your Bible. Take a moment and sketch out your idea for this entry using one of the Margin Templates and if you are comfortable, go ahead and add it into your Bible.

CHAPTER SEVEN

Pen To Paper

I went to kindergarten when it was still *just* kindergarten. The teachers weren't so worried about our readiness for the first grade. They were more focused on important things like sharing and music and naps and my personal favorite . . . art!

Oh how I loved to hear Mrs. Knox say, *"It's time for art—go get your smocks on!"* We would all hustle over to our cubbies to grab our "smocks"—which were really just some of our Dads' old shirts that we put on backwards. Mrs. Knox would button them at the collar for us. Mine was covered in bright colors and handprints—I guess that white shirt must have looked like another canvas to me, crying out to be painted upon. And of course, I obliged!

I've waited through six whole chapters to be able to say this to you: *"It's time for art—go get your smocks on!"*

Tools and Supplies—Rather than take up room here in the chapter, I have included some information about my favorite tools and supplies in the Resource section at the end of the book, but I do want to cover a couple of things before we move on.

Regardless of what kind of Journaling Bible you choose to use, you need to keep in mind that the paper used in Bible printing is about as different as it can get from any kind of art paper you may have ever used before. It will be thinner. It may be coated. The paper in your Bible wasn't selected by the publisher because of how well it works with paint and inks, so you will need to test any supplies you plan to use—even if you have seen someone else use them with beautiful results.

There is enough variance between the paper found in different Bibles, as well as the way a journaler uses a certain product that you do not want to assume you will get the same results. I can't emphasize this enough. I have dedicated the last few pages in my Bible as a test kitchen of sorts.

Because I teach workshops, I have needed to try out a wide variety of inks, pens, paints and markers. In this picture you can see I have created labels based on the type of ink, pen or marker I was going to test. I used it on the page without any sealer because I wanted to know what the paper would do when it came in contact with the product. Some bled through immediately, some did not. And just because it bled through, that didn't mean I would never use it. I just know that if I want or need to use that product, I must *seal*[40] the page prior to using it. Testing for yourself is an important thing to do to ensure that you will like what you create—so just plan on it, please.

Meeting Your Journaling Bible For The First Time

If you are like me, the first time you open your Journaling Bible may be both an exciting and daunting experience. I couldn't wait. After tearing open the box and removing the shrink-wrap (dare I mention that I brought it up to my face to smell that wonderful new book smell?), I lovingly let the pages fall open to some place in the middle and set it down. Then I promptly thought, *"Oh my, how pristine you are!"* And it was.

Unlike my study Bible, it had not a single mark upon its pages. Nothing was underlined or noted. I'm pretty sure there were no fingerprints on it other than mine. And while my fingers were itching to get started, my mind was hit with a severe case of *blank canvas syndrome.*

If you have never suffered from *blank canvas syndrome*, it can be a bit overwhelming and you may find yourself thinking, *"I better come up with something pretty spectacular to put in here for my first entry!"* If you aren't careful or haven't been warned, you may walk away and stay away for a while because you simply cannot imagine doing anything until it is absolutely *perfect.*

The very best thing to do is to make it just a touch less pristine. I'm not suggesting that you spill your coffee on it or anything like that, but I do have some ideas that will allow you to *start* without feeling the pressure of creating a perfect first page.

Add tabs to mark the books of the Bible. This is certainly a personal preference, but it is an easy way to add something to your Bible that immediately makes it feel a bit more like *yours*. If you do not want to add tabs, another thing that many Bible journalers do is to put a strip of washi tape over the edge of the first page of each book. This removable decorative tape adds some color to the edge of your Bible, making that page just a little thicker so it is easier to find as you are thumbing through the pages.

Decorate your "This Book Belongs To" *page*. I've seen lots of journalers doing this and am always inspired by how they have put their personal touch on this very first page. My friend, the very talented Jamie Dougherty, created this

beautiful page for her Bible[41] and has given me permission to share it with you. If you would like to use her line art to create your own "*This Book Belongs To*" page, you will find the link in the Resource section at the back of the book. This is a great way begin and is such a beautiful way to lay claim to your Bible.

Create a purpose or permissions page in the front or back of your Bible. These can be simple statements that you use to remind yourself what your plans or intentions are for this Bible. You don't have to have this all figured out the first time you open it   . . . and if you are doing the *21 Day Experiment*, this could be a place where you write about the experiences or specific things you have learned. By writing them here, you can refer to them often and affirm that you are sticking with those things you have determined will provide you with the best experience.

One of the best "permissions" pages I have seen was by Lauren from the blog, *The Thinking Closet*[42]. She has written

in very loose painted script: *"This Bible is for (hearing God's voice, keeping it real, worshiping through art, sloppy handwriting, messy imperfect efforts, in-process thoughts, brokenness and others); This Bible is NOT for (perfection, proving how spiritual I am, neat tidy thoughts, showing off my mad art skills and others) and these pages may (wrinkle, crinkle, bleed, curl, be ugly, rrriiiiiippppp, get stained, get started and not finished and others)."* Sometimes the only thing we need to stop being paralyzed is to give up the illusion that perfection is required and achievable . . . especially since it is neither.

I promise, once you've made the first mark in your Bible, the rest will come much more easily.

The important thing is to start!

Your First Entry

You are probably already asking yourself, *"Where do I begin?"* Of course the answer is: *anywhere you like*!

Again, in the early stages of journaling in your Bible, these feel like momentous decisions—and of course they are. But you need not stress or lose sleep over them. My best suggestion is for you to do one of two things.

Begin by doing a favorite verse or perhaps your life verse. There are conversations I wish we could have in person because if we were together and I saw that you were particularly nervous about choosing where to begin, I would have you stand up and walk around the room shaking out your arms and breathing deeply.

Also, you might try listening to Taylor Swift's song, *Shake it Off*[43]—it helps. When you've done that, it is usually hard to take yourself too seriously. And while the choice of where to begin does deserve some consideration, in reality, any verse that you choose will be a good one.

I often suggest using a favorite verse as a place to begin because you have already lived with it for a while . . . the reflection and tarrying has been happening as you've gone about living your life, so you can move right into journaling about it.

The other thing I often suggest is to ***begin where you are currently studying***. If you are going to use this as part of your regular devotion or study routine, then when you are ready—just add it in. That is what I did. Because I think of *Illuminated Journaling* as a tool to use in my study time, I have just treated it like another reference book that is on my pile of books to use when I need it. I reach for my Journaling Bible very often now because it has proven to be a most useful tool—and I'm sure yours will be for you as well.

Defining Your Style

I smile as I type these words because I know that when I first began journaling, my style was about as well defined as that of a young girl playing *dress up*. My sister, Robyn, and I loved to dress up in our Mom's clothes—and we were *quite* the creative fashionistas! I'm sure it made our mother shiver when she  saw some of the outfits we put together. We certainly hadn't seen her put *that* hat with   *that* dress!

But that is both the fun and horror of discovering your style: some things will work well, while others—not so much. But it is all okay.

One day you may look back on some of your pages and say, *"What was I thinking?"* I certainly have. But even those less than perfect pages will tell the story of what was happening between you and God at that moment.

So go ahead! Try some of these styles on and see if you like them.

Hand Lettered

Almost from the first day I began journaling in my Bible, I have been drawn to the way hand lettering can focus the viewer's eye onto the   portion of a verse or quote that you want to set apart for emphasis[44]. This is one of the best ways to begin because the only things you really need are a pencil, a white eraser, and a black pen.

If you need some examples to work from—Pinterest™ has the idea mother lode. Not only can you find examples of hand lettering in Journaling Bibles, but a quick search on the word *font* or *typography* will give you thousands of examples to print out and use as a guide. I have created a Pinterest Board called *Cool Typography* and you are welcome to stop by for some inspiration. It contains links to free typography examples that you can download and some great font combinations that I often use myself.

Modern Collage

Modern Collage is a very fresh style with no right or wrong way of doing it. The general plan is scrape thin layers of paint (usually acrylic) onto the page and then add stickers, stamps, bits of paper, tags, labels, washi tape, journaling and even a few splatters of paint—all of which create the focal image to communicate the journaler's point.

It may sound scary—scraping acrylic paint—but as you can see in my "O Lord!" page[45], even heavy-bodied acrylic is transparent when you  scrape it thinly across the page. I use an old hotel key card and end up putting most of the paint back in the bottle or onto another page because this easy technique doesn't use very much paint at all.

There is something very freeing about working on an entry with this style. I tend to use bolder colors than I might normally be drawn to and I like the process of adding bits and pieces together to make the whole page look more beautiful than those individual things would have looked alone.

Whenever I work on one of these pages, I am reminded of the passage in 1 Corinthians where Paul admonishes us: *"As it is, there are many parts, yet one body.*" Christ's followers are walking examples of modern collage—together we give a better picture of Christ than we do by ourselves.

Again, Pinterest™ is a great place to go look for some inspiration. I would also suggest Instagram™ as more and more Bible journalers have begun posting their pages there. I have listed some of my favorite posters in the Resource section of the book, as well as some great hashtags to use to find others.

Focal Image

This is probably my favored style for my own journaling. I am drawn to how an image has the ability to make a strong statement, or to express a small nuance in less space than

all the words I would need to communicate the same thing[46].

There are many ways to add an image to your page. A few that I like to use are stamping, sketching or creating line art for a transfer.

If you are not confident in your drawing ability (I certainly wasn't when I started) you can use tracing paper, graphite paper and a pencil to copy a picture from a magazine, Google™ image or one of your own photos. Depending on where you find your image, you can resize it to fit onto your page by using photo editing software—or you can go "old school" and resize it with a copy machine. Once you have the basic lines sketched in, use your reference photo to guide you as you add color and shading to the image.

If I am going to use one of my own drawings, I start in a sketchbook. That way I can work on it and erase as much as I need to without wearing the paper thin in my Bible. Once I feel good about the drawing, I use the same method of tracing it and using graphite paper to add the line art into my Bible.

When I am working with a focal image, I like to add the line art to the page, and then also add my title before I start adding color with paint or colored pencils. Both elements are so important and I want to make sure they balance each other out.

There are countless ways to add color to your focal image. My personal favorite combines watercolor and colored pencils. Soon after I started journaling in my Bible, I discovered that putting down several thin layers of watercolor and drying them in between kept other things from bleeding through the pages quite as badly. It didn't really make sense, but I came to the conclusion that I didn't have to understand it to be glad that it worked. That's the thing about working in your Journaling Bible: it sometimes defies what you think it will do, so you just have to test it for yourself.

I really do love using colored pencils too. I loved coloring geography maps with them in school—I just felt so grown up to have moved from crayons to colored pencils. I like that you can sharpen them to a fine point and that they blend well on top of watercolor. The two mediums, when combined, give a very finished look to focal images . . . and you can get great results without having a lot of experience.

I teach this technique in all of my live workshops because it is so much fun to watch new Bible journalers discover that they really love what they have just created—even though they had been saying they didn't have a creative bone in their body. *Mmm Hmmm . . . they can't say that anymore!*

These are merely a few styles—and I know my descriptions have been brief—but I just want to give you a few ideas to get you started. You may end up using a hybrid of these or creating one of your own. I would highly recommend that you go to Pinterest™, Facebook™ and

Instagram™ and see what appeals to you . . . do a little virtual window shopping.

I would also suggest that you consider taking a class or two, particularly if you are a visual learner. Watching how someone else creates can help you skip over many mistakes for yourself. I offer free Tutorials and in-depth online Workshops on IlluminatedJournaling.com—and there are a lot of other teachers with really terrific classes to help you get started as well.

The Goal Is Not Perfection

I know I keep repeating myself, but it's kind of important. The goal is not *perfection*, but *reflection*!

As a Bible journaler, the need for perfection is not your friend. Here is what perfection will get you:

> *Perfection* steals your joy.
> *Perfection* paralyzes.
> *Perfection* compares your work to others and says,
>   "*You don't measure up.*"
> *Perfection* tries to convince you that it is your abilities
>   that make your offering acceptable to God—instead
>   of the truth that your offering is acceptable because
>   you are a child of the King, covered by the blood
>   of Jesus.
> *Perfection* changes tarrying into toiling.
> *Perfection* makes you give up.

Just like any new skill, there is a learning curve. Accept that there are going to be mistakes and accidents. You can recover from just about anything. Blobs of paint can make beautiful flowers. A slip of the pen can be turned into a flourished embellishment. When accidents happen, we just have to get creative and find a way to incorporate them into our page.

Strive to give God your best, but give perfection a rest!

But it isn't enough to set aside your need for perfection. We need to replace it with something better. Reflection is not only better—it's great!

Reflection celebrates your joy.
Reflection brings new discoveries.
Reflection knows that your creativity comes from God.
Reflection changes you first and *then* the world.
Reflection brings peace and understanding.
Reflection urges you to try again.
Reflection says, *"You're good enough."*
Reflection is filled with grace.
Reflection buttons the collar when you put your smock
      on and says, *"Give it a go and have fun!"*

Illumination

Let's do a little brainstorming.

Next to each of these styles, write a scripture passage or a quote that would lend itself to being journaled in that style. For instance, next to *Focal Image,* I might write *Psalm 23* because I can imagine all sorts of illustrations that would use the imagery found in the verses to communicate my own need for a shepherd. So now it's your turn.

Hand Lettering:

Modern Collage:

Focal Image:

Was one of these styles easier to think of a verse for than the others? Which one? Why?

This isn't a totally scientific methodology, but if you are trying to figure out which style to try first, you might consider going with the one that was the easiest for you to imagine using.

Click Stop

Consider using one of the style/Bible passage pairings that you wrote down. Jot down a few notes to use later.

Take some time to tarry with it. Ask God for creativity as you think about it—and when you feel like you have a good direction, sketch out your idea using a Margin Template or a separate journal. If you are comfortable doing so, set aside some time to try your hand at journaling this passage into your Bible in the style you have selected.

Remember: it doesn't have to be perfect. This is just an experiment in finding your style. You are going to be blessed to have taken the time to add this into your Journaling Bible regardless of how well you execute the style.

Now go get your smock on . . . it's time for art!

CHAPTER EIGHT

It's Refrigerator Worthy

I have a few quirks. That's not remarkable. But what *is* remarkable is that I *admit* I have them!

Oh yes, I see that gleam in your eye! You think I am going to tell you what they are. Oh okay, but just a couple of them because I don't want to ruin what you might think of me or tarnish my sterling reputation.

When my sister, Robyn, and I play the board game *Trouble*™ with the kids, we go out of our way not to send the other one "home." Of course, that same courtesy does *not* extend to any child over the age of twelve. Now before you go on the hunt for the name of a good counselor for me, I have one. She has set me straight on many things. But even she says this is just one of the quirky things about me . . . well, and my sister too. We have been the best of friends since we were little girls and we just choose not to compete with each other on this one game.

Who knows why? We just don't. We're quirky like that.

And here's one more: whenever I am talking with someone—in my mind—*I always think we are about the same age.* If I am talking to a grandma, I can feel my bones aching and I find myself nodding in agreement about "how things were back in the good old days." Wait . . . I actually *am* the same age as a grandmother. *Never mind.*

But the same thing happens when I sit down on the floor with a child and a coloring book. I feel my spirit lighten and my fingers begin to twitch as I anticipate which color I am going to choose to use first—it's so hard to choose if you actually get to use the sixty-four color box!

And then a remarkable thing happens. As we get close to finishing, I start thinking about where on the refrigerator we are going to hang our pictures. I am transported back to what it was like to be five years old and utterly convinced that when you finished a piece of art, of course your mom was going to give it a place of honor on the refrigerator door.

Of course—it's refrigerator worthy!

Oh to be able to hold on to that mindset when I approach journaling in my Bible.

> *Lord, please help me to come to You like a child! When I bring an offering of praise in the form of a journaling Bible entry, help me approach You with wonder, confidence and absolute trust that You have reserved a place for it on whatever is the equivalent of heaven's refrigerator door. And Lord, more importantly, please help me to encourage this dear reader that You eagerly anticipate meeting with them on the pages of Your Word and can't wait to see how they respond to Your time together when they journal about it!*
> *Thank You so much!*
> *Amen*

In my heart, I believe this may be the most important chapter in this book. As I am writing, I can look up on the wall in front of my desk and see a list of people's names I keep in mind as I am writing. They would probably be surprised to know that their names are on my list because I have never met any of them face to face. In fact, as I work on this chapter, none of them even know I am writing a book. But they are the reason that I have felt so compelled to sit down and write.

I chose them because I have been touched by their personal testimonies of what journaling in their Bible has done for them. I have the names of a mother and a daughter who have reconciled because they opened the Word of God together and found the path back to each other. I have the name of a teenager who is the only Christ follower in her family and for whom journaling is a tangible connection point in a faith walk that can be lonely in her circumstances. I have the name of a woman who is using journaling to help her walk through the first year of living life without her husband who has gone home to be with the Lord. And I have several other names of people who have simply expressed that they want to know Jesus more, to serve Him better and to let God's Word be the standard by which they lead their lives.

All of them have expressed that journaling in their Bible is helping them to do that—and my greatest desire is to help add to their number by making *Illuminated Journaling* easy and approachable for anyone to do . . . and with the sure belief that they too will see the Word of God accomplish marvelous and miraculous things in their lives. *I want that for you in your life!* And this is the chapter where I want to address the thing that can help make journaling in your Bible a life changing pursuit and not just a cool idea you saw on social media and decided to try for a while.

What you do in your Bible is between you and God. Let me say that again. Regardless of the fact that most of us discovered *Illuminated Journaling* via social media, this is not something we do for the eyes of others. It is about what happens between you and God in the quiet of your study and how you choose to respond back to Him in your journal.

There is no place for comparison or competition . . . *none.*

There are countless other artists whose skills are greater than mine—and I love learning from them. But the minute I start comparing what I am capable of doing to what I see them do, I begin to question if my offering is going to be good enough for God. Surely He would prefer to give the place of honor to their page, not mine. Surely, He can't help but turn to Jesus and say, *"Wow, now there's an artist!"*

No, He doesn't. *Not. Ever.*

If you have been a Christ follower for a long time, you know the right answers. When asked if God loves you as much as He loves someone like Sister Theresa, you know to say, *"God loves us all the same."* If you are a new child of the King or you are just seeking to find out what Christianity is all about, the answers may not come as quickly.

But either way, if you are older than about eleven years, there is a good chance you've lost some degree of believing that your offering is "refrigerator worthy." It happens because life tends to crush that confident spirit we have as children, particularly in regards to our creative expression. We become timid and fearful of making mistakes.

Because a mistake would render our offering *less than.*

Our hearts so long to see the look of love and approval upon the face of God when we hand Him our gift, so we mistakenly think that the look of love and approval will only come if we somehow figure out how to do enough things right to deserve His love. But that just isn't how God works, even if our feelings try to convince us otherwise. It's just not His plan—He knows we can never be good enough. His way makes it possible, not our way.

You, dear reader, are precious in the sight of God and it is important that you know a few very important truths!

[47]He knows your name.[48]

Jesus died for you and me when we didn't deserve it. The fifth chapter of Romans focuses our attention on just how remarkable that is. "*. . . Christ died for the ungodly. For one will scarcely die for a   righteous person—though perhaps for a good person one would dare even to die— but God shows his love for us in that while we were still sinners, Christ died for us.*"[49]

Because of His sacri-fice on the cross—His death, burial and resur-rection—we are no longer under a sentence of death. *For God so loved the world that He gave His only Son, that whoever believes in Him should not perish but have eternal life*[50].

He says that He has you inscribed on the palms of His hands.[51] Do you know that He sees your face when He

glances down at His nail-scarred hands? He sees *your* face and is glad He made the sacrifice. Do you know He did all of this so that we can be bold when we approach Him? We don't have to slink in on our bellies, eyes cast down, heads bowed, crying "unclean" like lepers used to do in ancient times.

No. We have become His sons and daughters. Children of the King![52] It is a gift freely given—but we have to accept it.

Dear reader, if as you read this chapter, you have felt in your heart you are not certain that your sins have been forgiven, I don't want to go any further without offering you a gift: the opportunity to accept Jesus as your Savior. It is such a simple prayer and you can pray it right now.

Dear Lord Jesus,

I know I am a sinner, and I ask for Your forgiveness. I believe You died for my sins and rose from the dead. I trust and follow You as my Lord and Savior. Guide my life and help me to do Your will.

In Your Name, Amen.

If you were not yet ready to ask Jesus to be your Savior, but you want to know more, please look for the brief article called *The Plan of Salvation* that I have placed in the Resource section at the end of the book.

Perhaps you already know Jesus as your Savior—but you struggle with feelings of guilt and condemnation. You may be trying to pay God back for what you've done wrong—when Jesus already made it right. God's unconditional love is a very difficult concept for people to accept because, in the world, there's always payment for everything we receive. It's just how things work here. But God is not like people!

Aren't you glad about that?

We need to learn that whether or not we feel forgiven, we are forgiven. Accepting that will make it much easier to take your offering to God. Knowing that He is as excited to see you, as you are to see Him will put a skip in your step . . . even if you have to lean on your walker to do it.

There is nothing more important than having these issues settled in your heart and mind once and for all. When the weight is lifted off your shoulders, you will find so much more joy in the times when you meet with God on the pages of your Bible.

You will come to wait expectantly on His answers, rather than dreading what He might have to say to you. Even if you, like me, have known Him for a long time, it is still good to stop and refresh our minds with the truth that He loves us . . . unconditionally.

And just like I told you about those few names up on the wall in front of my desk that remind me why I am writing this book, He has every one of our names on the tip of His tongue—and always on His mind. You need to have no fear that there will not be a spot on His refrigerator for your gift. It's already been reserved.

And while I haven't seen it personally yet, I hear it is ginormous! Go put your smock on, pull out that sixty-four box of crayons, get in touch with your five-year-old self and get busy—He can't wait to see what you will bring Him next!

Illumination

I love stories, don't you? I can entertain myself for hours sitting in an airport, waiting for my flight to leave. Even if I only have a few minutes, I like picking out one or two people who find themselves waiting as well and tell myself a story about them. It's not that hard. Everyone has a story and I like imagining what might have happened just before I saw them, where they are going or what is going to happen to them after they get there . . . wherever "there" is.

I hope you will indulge me just a bit because I would like to tell you a story. I call it: *Mary And Her Gift of Oil.* It is loosely based upon what the Bible tells us about Mary and her family[53]—but of course, I've added a few of the details I've imagined when I met them on the pages of my Bible.

Mary lives in Bethany with her brother and sister—I don't recall their last name. All three of them love Jesus—and He loves them back. Jesus often comes to stay at their house and, inevitably, the neighbors all come over to hear Him teach. And, just as inevitably, the neighbors usually stay right through suppertime . . . and not one of them ever thinks to bring a covered dish.

But that's okay. Mary's sister, Martha, loves to cook for Jesus and all of her neighbors. But she sure could use a little help the day I meet them. She doesn't mind that no one has brought a green bean casserole or a red velvet cake—but she is *none too happy* with her sister. As far as Martha is concerned, Mary hasn't done one thing to help her.

In fact, she can't think when she saw her last. She ponders that for a moment, trying to remember what she asked Mary to do before she disappeared. Then it comes to her. *"I asked her an hour ago to go to the well and bring back some water—and she is still not back. What has that girl gotten into? These dishes aren't going to clean themselves!"*

She begins to stomp around the kitchen, the words she mutters match the rhythm of her stomps. *"You* [step] *would* [step] *think* [step] *that* [step] *she* [step] *could* [step] *manage* [step] [step] *to* [step] *do* [step] *one* [step] *thing* [step]*—just one!* [step] [step]*!"*

A burst of laughter from the other room breaks her train of thought and stops her in her tracks. Mixed in with the sound of male laughter comes a lone female's laugh—a laugh she has known all her life. It is Mary. *"Oh for goodness sakes! She's in there with Jesus!"* A quick peek from the doorway confirms what Martha already knows: Mary is seated at the feet of Jesus, her water buckets filled to the rim sitting right beside her.

Martha whirls around and heads back to the kitchen, muttering all the way, *"It's not like I wouldn't like to be in there listening to Jesus, too! But then, what would the neighbors says? I'm sure Jesus is embarrassed too . . . she is the only woman in there. It has to have made Him uncomfortable. And even though I would never want Him to mention it, He is probably thinking that Mary should be in here helping me!"* Martha finishes up in the kitchen talking to herself the whole time, waiting for the meeting in the other room to break up so she can apologize to Jesus for her sister's poor manners.

Meanwhile, Mary is sitting on the floor listening to Jesus talk about what heaven will be like. She can't help but think, *"When Jesus describes heaven, it's like He has been there!"* She leans in to listen more intently and her hand accidentally brushes one of the buckets and it causes a little splash. It soaks into her skirt.

"Oh dear, Martha is not going to be happy with me," she thinks. *"I wish she would come in here—she would just love to hear about the place that Jesus says He will have waiting for us when we get to heaven. It would make her so happy to hear that she is going to have a mansion—and she won't even have to clean it! I have to remember to tell her about that . . . but I'll probably have to wait until she finishes fussing at me for forgetting to bring her this water. Oh well, she probably can't get any more angry than she already is, so I might as well stay and hear what else Jesus has to say."*

And, when the teaching time is over, Mary stands, lifts the buckets and heads into the kitchen to do the dishes. Sure enough, they are still there stacked in the sink waiting for her arrival. She sees Martha drying her hands on her skirt and waiting to get Jesus' attention now that He is done . . . and although she knows it is too much to hope for, she indeed hopes that all they are going to talk about is the mansion Jesus is preparing in heaven for Martha!

[Storyteller's Pause] As you are no doubt aware, Jesus didn't get to talk to Martha about the mansion as Mary had hoped He would. Martha just couldn't help herself and blurted out, *"Lord, do you not care that my sister has left me to serve alone? Tell her then to help me."* And much to her surprise, Jesus didn't shake His head and agree with her that it just wasn't right for

Mary to leave her to take care of all the supper preparations and clean up all by herself. Instead, He put His arm around her shoulders and said, *"Martha, Martha, you are anxious and troubled about many things, but one thing is necessary. Mary has chosen the good portion, which will not be taken away from her."* But *the way* He said it took the sting from His words and Martha felt her frustration with her sister begin to melt away. She even formed a tiny new thought about the next time Jesus would came to stay—perhaps she would let the dishes wait and go and sit with Mary at His feet.

Now you may be thinking to yourself, *"I thought Jann said this story was about Mary—it seemed a bit more focused on Martha than Mary."* I'm glad you mentioned that because I wanted you to get to know a little about Mary and Martha together. You see, the next part of the story might seem a bit strange if you don't know what had happened before and why it didn't seem to bother Martha or cause her to step in and stop her sister. Apparently, she took Jesus' words to heart and was more focused on honoring Jesus with her presence than getting the mess cleaned up while He taught—but that's another story altogether.

A few months later, Jesus came back to Bethany and it was just six days before Passover. A lot has happened since we saw them last. Mary and Martha's brother, Lazarus, had become very ill and had died. The sisters had tried to get word to Jesus about Lazarus—hoping that He would get there in time to heal their brother—but He was too late. Obviously, they were heartbroken. Jesus was extremely sad too and He went to visit the tomb where Lazarus was buried. He went in alone, but when He came out, Lazarus came out with Him! Jesus had raised Lazarus from the dead. And *that's another story altogether as well*, but I will save it for another day.

But on this occasion, Jesus returned to Mary and Martha's house six days before Passover—just six days before He would go to Jerusalem to be arrested and crucified. Of course, they had supper—no doubt celebrating the fact that Lazarus was alive and well enough to host another gathering of neighbors around the table. But at the end of the supper, Mary slipped into the room carrying a jar filled with expensive oil called *Nard*.

Martha was watching her sister—knowing what she was about to do and how much they both wanted it to be received well by Jesus. She was no longer concerned about what the neighbors might think—but she did pray that Jesus would understand all that their gift was meant to communicate.

They had talked for weeks about what they could do to show how much they loved Jesus, believing that He was the Messiah they had been waiting for. They desired to thank Him for bringing their brother back from the dead. But there just didn't seem to be *anything* that could possibly convey all that they felt about Jesus.

And then, Mary had an idea. While they were clearing away the breakfast dishes the week before, Mary had asked Martha if she had noticed that Jesus had been talking a lot more about His own death the last few times He had come to visit. Martha hadn't really noticed it until Mary said something about it, but they both were able to think of several times that the conversation had turned to the topic of what it would be like when Jesus was no longer with them. It made everyone a little uncomfortable, but when someone would try to change the subject, Jesus was quick to return to what He had been saying.

The more Mary and Martha thought about it, the more they became convinced that Jesus had been trying to tell all of His followers He wasn't going to be with them much longer. That made their hearts all the heavier as they went about preparing for His visit on His way to Jerusalem for the Passover . . . and *that* was when they figured out what they wanted to do.

They wanted to anoint Jesus for burial *before* He died and while He was still staying there in their family's home. The more they thought and talked about it, the more certain they became. They finally put their plan in action and went to purchase the oil. They didn't even tell Lazarus what they were going to do, not that he would have stopped them.

So when Martha saw Mary step into the room carrying the jar of oil, she almost quit breathing. The old Martha might have been worried about the cost of the oil or what the neighbors might say, but that girl was gone. This Martha was just so grateful for the opportunity to express to Jesus how much she and her sister loved Him that she didn't have another thought in the world. And from the look on her sister's face, Mary didn't either.

Mary didn't even see the heads of her brother's guest turn as she slipped into the room. She had stopped caring long ago what they thought about her. Her eyes were fixed on Jesus and she knew that the scent from the precious oil she was carrying was filling the room. It was a scent everyone associated with death. Nard was used to anoint bodies at the time of their burial—and it seemed out of place in this room where all the guests were resting after a delicious meal.

Mary moved to the head of the table where Jesus was reclined. She didn't even notice the scowl she was getting from one of Jesus' disciples, Judas. She just knelt at the feet of Jesus and began anointing His feet with the oil from her jar. The minute she took the lid off the jar, the whole house was filled with the scent. In fact, it was so strong that anyone walking by the house would think that the family had recently lost a loved one..

The disciple who had been so obviously displeased when Mary came into the room spoke up. *"Why was this ointment not sold for three hundred denarii and given to the poor?"* he asked.

Martha rolled her eyes. *"Of course Mr. Moneybags would ask that."* But she was most interested in how Jesus was going to answer him. That would tell her if Jesus truly understood why she and Mary had spent all of their savings to purchase this jar of oil.

Jesus didn't disappoint. *"Leave her alone, so that she may keep it for the day of my burial. For the poor you always have with you, but you do not always have me."*

Mary finished anointing Jesus' feet and wiped away the excess with her hair. She quietly stood and left the room with tears streaming down her cheeks. When she got to where Martha was waiting in the doorway, she reached out for her sister 's hand and together they walked back to another room where they could hug each other closely. They wept quietly. They had heard what Jesus said to Judas. His words affirmed what they had thought—this was most likely the last time they would ever get to be with Jesus while He was alive and they couldn't imagine their lives without Him.

When I read the Bible, I try and see the people in the stories as real live flesh and blood human beings—who have lived real lives prior to and after we see them on the pages of the Word. I don't really know if the things that I imagined about Mary and Martha were completely accurate—the Bible doesn't tell us. But I know they did live real lives, had real feelings, struggled with real character flaws and did really love Jesus . . . just like I do.

If you were to cast yourself as one of the characters in my story—who would it be? Do you identify with Mary or Martha? Maybe you didn't see yourself in either one of them. Maybe you were more like the neighbors who couldn't wait to come to supper and hear Jesus. Or perhaps you feel more like Lazarus because Jesus has taken you from a life headed to the grave and has given you a new life instead. Or did Judas' words ring more true to you?

For myself—if I am honest—there are bits of each of these characters within me. I have some of their worst traits and some of their best. The only thing that redeems my personal story is Jesus.

Take a moment and jot a few thoughts that occur to you about the role you would have played in this story.

Click Stop

Take a moment and re-read what you just wrote.

Keeping in mind that whatever you create will be refrigerator worthy—consider doing something very special when you journal about what you have learned from *Mary and Her Gift Of Oil.*

Mary and Martha's gift cost all of their savings. Could you consider giving a gift in your journaling Bible that requires you to take a chance?

Sketch out what that might be . . . be bold. This is between you and God. No one else ever needs to see it.

When you are comfortable, execute your plan and share it with the Lord. He has a place reserved for it—and for you—on His ginormous refrigerator!

CHAPTER NINE

Sharing Your heART

If you could see me right now, you would see a woman who's heart is so full that it is leaking out the corner of her eyes.

When I began writing about *Illuminated Journaling*, I did so with just the beginning of a picture of you in my mind. I have seen glimpses of who you may be in my Instagram™ feed and in my Facebook™ groups. And I may even have some of your art pinned on my Pinterest™ boards. I've been inspired by your art and challenged by your heart for God. I've begun to think of what we do when we post one of our journaling pages on social media as sharing our *heART*— because it is such a unique blend of the two.

As I have been privileged to set aside time to write about how *Illuminated Journaling* has changed my walk with the Lord, God has brought my picture of you into clearer focus. You have been on His heart—and He has reminded me of that every time I have begun to write.

We've talked about you, He and I. Of course, He knows you much better than I do and I've tried to listen closely to His counsel in deciding what to include here and what should be left for another time. There is one more topic He has been pressing me to share with you—and I've saved it for last.

When You Share, Take Care

The last few months, we have seen an explosion of people beginning to journal in their Bibles. Social media has been the vehicle to introduce thousands of people to a new way to approach the Word of God via journaling onto the pages of their Bible. It is remarkable. Only God could have spread the word this quickly.

And the results are miraculous. People who had thought there was nothing for them in organized religion have found a way to approach God on the pages of their Bible and their faith has been restored. Lives have been changed. Relationships have been reconciled. New friendships have been formed. People who have felt cut off from fellowshipping with other Christ followers because of health or geography have found like-minded communities they can participate in from their homes. People have come to know Christ for the very first time.

Amazing, amazing things.

It has been a real-time example of Isaiah 55:11. *"So shall my word be that goes out from my mouth; it shall not return to me empty, but it shall accomplish that which I purpose, and shall succeed in the thing for which I sent it."* [54] Clearly, as the Word has gone out into the world, it has not returned empty and has certainly accomplished the purpose for which He sent it.

I know from personal experience that there have been posts I have shared because I felt impressed that someone other than myself might be able to relate to what I had expressed through the imagery and accompanying short devotional. And even though I had felt led by God to do so, frankly I was overwhelmed by the number of people who took the time to tell me about the impact my post had on them. When I heard their stories, it made me look at my post in a different light. Even though I only put things into my Bible that directly result from my time in the Word, God can and has purposed it to accomplish things other than just what it does for me.

Doesn't that just blow your mind?

It does mine! Journaling is so very personal and specific to my relationship with God that when I am working on a page, it feels like there could be no one else that it would apply to . . . but it sometimes does. That is because when His Word is sent out, it never returns empty. Only God could find a way to take something so personal and re-communicate it in a universal way. Can you tell that even though I've seen Him do it time and again, I still just scratch my head and say, *"How do you do that?"*

Clearly it has been God's plan to take this surge from social media to move His agenda forward. There is so much that is discouraging and causes our hearts to tremble at the temerity of people who think they can jeer and mock all that is good and holy and not face any consequences. Seeing a post where one of you has shared your heART standing in stark contrast to the darkness that is so often the norm makes me want to stand up and cheer! "Yes, Lord!"

Light casts out darkness . . . darkness can never overcome the light.

But I have also received emails from dear ones whose hearts have been wounded. They have shared their heART and someone they've never even met felt the freedom to verbally attack them or dismiss their testimony as irrelevant. You may have experience that too. Or worse, someone you love may speak dark words into your ears that make their way into your heart.

"You draw like a child."

"Why would you put that out there? I'd be embarrassed."

"No one cares . . . you've got nothing to say that anyone would want to hear."

"If people really knew you, they wouldn't think you were all that holy!"

I don't need to repeat the words. If dark words have been spoken to you, they are easily recalled. If you have heard those words, *I am so very sorry.*

Your Heavenly Father has heard them too. He has seen your spirit crushed . . . and He has seen how it was just a little bit harder for you to continue to respond to Him without inhibition the next time you sat down to work in your Bible.

Some of this heartache we just cannot avoid. We live in a fallen world and there are plenty of folks who can't wait to take a swipe at one of God's children. They think they are safe, but in actuality, as my grandmother used to say, they don't have the sense God gave a turnip!

I'm probably old enough to be your grandmother, so would you allow me to share some grandmotherly advice?

When it comes to sharing the most tender parts of our heART, we need to be careful not to "cast our pearls before swine."[55] If there is something you are still processing, be very careful where you share it. I'm not saying this to discourage you from sharing—not at all. But when we are still in the midst of a battle or trying to find solid ground in the midst of a storm, not everyone's comments will be helpful or appreciated. In fact, they can set us back or make us feel like we've had our feet knocked out from under us. Better to share it in a very safe environment or wait until we have our feet firmly planted under us before we let everyone in the world have access to the things that have the potential to wound us the most.

There are things in my Bible I do not share. I'm not sure I will ever share them on social media, but I know that for now, I need to protect my heART by not granting access to someone who doesn't necessarily know me or have my best interests at heart. I am blessed to have family and a friend or two who are close enough that I can share these kinds of things with them with the confidence they will gladly give me either a pat on the back or a kick in the butt—depending upon which one I really need!

That being said, there are many "closed" groups on Facebook that have specifically kept the walls up a bit so that those who participate can feel reasonably safe to share what they have been journaling in their Bible. These closed groups are not trying to be stand-offish when they require you to request to be a part of them. It is merely a way to make sure all who participate do so for the right reasons. Some groups have grown to be very large—evidence that sharing in a safe environment is both an encouragement and a blessing.

I am not saying any of this to be discouraging. I think we have discovered a most excellent way to approach God with the deepest parts of our hearts and souls. I don't want anyone to lose heART because they have been mangled by the opinions of people who don't have the sense God gave a turnip.

Once you find yourself on solid ground, you will not be moved should someone try to hurl an insult or throw dark words your way. If you feel that God is leading you to share something He has brought you through, you should feel confident that He will make you strong enough to withstand whatever may come your way. Your strength to share the hard times will be an encouragement to someone else. But know this, dear one: God does not wish you to be destroyed in order that someone else can be encouraged. His plans are to bring light and healing to you both.

Fortunately, much of what we want to share isn't based on the difficulties of our lives—it comes from a place of praise for who God is and what He has done.

Ok . . . deep breath! One more cautionary note, and then we can move on.

One of the things I have loved the most about all the communities that have sprung up on social media surrounding journaling in our Bibles is the fact that they draw such a diverse crowd of people. It is wonderful to be surrounded by people whose experiences are different from mine. We may not have walked the same walk, but we *have* walked with the same walking Partner. There is more that unites us than divides us!

Of course, you now know that I think *we are all about the same age.* However, a quick look at the demographics has shown me that we, in fact, are not. We are different ages. We come from different countries. We use different Bibles. We attend different types of churches. We are varied in our ethnicities. Some have finished raising their family and others are just beginning.

And dare I mention this? We approach God on the pages of our Bibles in different ways. So my caution is this: please be sensitive to the fact that there is no reason for this to divide us. Presume that all will ask God how they may proceed in their Bible. We can be confident that the Holy Spirit will stir their hearts to make it right.

Because our preferences tend to be strong in this area, let us be even more cautious about expressing our opinions—erring always on the side of encouragement. It is wise even to refrain from sharing thoughts of "*I wouldn't . . .*or *"I couldn't . . ."* Your preferences will be clear by the posts *you* make.

One more deep breath . . . glad we got *that* out of the way.

I'm sure you are ready for me to move on too—and I have received the "good to go" sign from God as well. We may never have direct knowledge of it, but His eye is always on us and when others hurt His sons and daughters, it doesn't sit well with Him. As the Creator, He knows He gave them more sense than He gave a turnip—and one day, He will hold them accountable for the fact that they didn't use it.

Your heART As A Blessing

I'm certain we have only begun to see all the things that God intends to use this heARTform for in the coming years, but my mind has begun to be filled with ways we can bless others outside social media. I love to give personal gifts for birthdays and Christmas, but especially for baby and bridal showers, or as a special thank you when a friend has gone out of her way help me.

The gifts I have chosen to give have changed over the years, but I have often tried to find a way to give something handmade . . . and I think sharing a Journaling Bible could be something especially wonderful for a variety of occasions.

If you will indulge me, I want to share one last story. I have been thinking for some time about what I could do for a dear new friend of mine. Until a few months ago, I had never met her. She is a delightful lady who has blessed me beyond what I could have even known I needed. When I first started writing on this book, I worked on it late at night when I couldn't sleep, on airplanes as I traveled for work, or propped up in a hotel bed. As my grandmother used to say, it was "catch it when you can."

Then the publisher asked for a formal proposal. I took one look at the three pages of questions they sent and almost threw my hands up in the air. My schedule had me on the road from March until June, with only a day or two at a time back home. I told Royce that I could never get that much writing done in such a short amount of time. You probably don't know Royce, but "never" is a word that does not reside in his vocabulary. I thank God I have him in my life.

As he picked me up from the airport, he said, "*I'm not taking you home. I've arranged for you to go to a Bed and Breakfast . . . a little cottage for the next seven days. Barrett* (Weston's dog) *is going to go with you. Then I'll pick you up and take you to the airport for your conferences next week.*"

He had it all arranged . . . and it was just what I needed.

Dr. Vicky was my hostess. She is a lady that pays attention to detail. My meals were delicious. Her gardens provided me a place to stretch my legs and rest my brain. I was able to work undisturbed for all hours of the day and night. She never intruded, but if she saw me out wandering around, she would come out to chat for a few brief minutes. We quickly discovered that we were sisters in Christ—that we had both been college professors, and that we both loved to start our day in the Word with a cup of coffee.

My time was quickly over, but I left Dr. Vicky's place with a completed book proposal and a stained glass cross she makes for each of her guests at the cottage. I hung it up in my studio to remind me of God's provision—just what we need, right when we need it.

Several weeks later, we learned that this book was going to indeed be published, but we needed to get the manuscript finished pronto. No time to panic—I just needed to get to work. Royce called Dr. Vicky again. This time the cottage wasn't available. She already had guests booked. But, she thought about it and called him back. "I got to thinking," she said. "Since I know Jann and she really needs to get this book done, I would be happy for her to come up to the farmhouse and stay with me. She can have the second floor all to herself—and I'll make sure that she eats."

Again, God knew exactly what I needed.

I stayed for almost two weeks and I couldn't have done it without her. We had breakfast early each morning and then I would take my pot of coffee up to the room we had set up as a writing area. I would sip coffee and talk with God about what we needed to accomplish that day. Dr. Vicky kept me fortified with yummy fruit smoothie shakes with protein, and fed me delicious dinners with food from her garden. I slept when I needed to sleep and often stayed up writing long into the nights.

And Dr. Vicky also prayed for me.

When I leave this time, I will have the completed manuscript with me. Even typing the words "completed manuscript" just brings me to tears. Happy tears, not sad ones. Tears that come as I contemplate God's goodness and favor to me. Joyful tears because of Royce's belief in my ability to write it and his willingness to figure out how to help me get it done. Tears from remembering my sister's voice saying, "*Of course you need to write it—when can you start?*" She said it like it was a foregone conclusion that all I needed to do was start and the completion would take care of itself! Tears of thankfulness for my dear friends who sustained me with their love and prayers.

And tears of gratitude for Dr. Vicky and all the ways she made this completion possible.

I finally decided to take her a Journaling Bible. It seemed fitting. And I have done one page in it for her. She is artistic and will no doubt fill its pages with her own experience with God.

I did a picture of her farmhouse . . . that dormer window is the one I gazed out of when I would stand to stretch my legs and see what was going on in the outside world. As I looked out over her beautiful lawn, I prayed the Prayer of Jabez over Dr. Vicky and her homestead. In 1 Chronicles 4:10 Jabez asked God, *"Oh that You would bless me and expand my border, and that your hand might be with me, and that You would keep me from harm . . . and God granted his request."*[56]

I wanted my gift to be personal. Her gift was incredibly personal to me.

I can imagine finding equally marvelous reasons to give a "starter" Illuminated Journaling Bible as a gift.

I am looking forward to giving Journaling Bibles to new mamas.[57] A baby holds so much promise . . . and the mama has so many hopes, dreams and prayers for her new child—what a perfect place for her to capture them. I know I'm about to put the final period at the end of the final sentence in this book, but my heart is already becoming full for the next one.

I would love to help moms fill the pages of an *Illuminated Legacy Bible* with all of the things they have prayed over their children:

> Letters written for birthdays,
> Prayers and the answers God provides for all the struggles
>   that will inevitably come into the life of the child,
> Promises God has showed her of His plans,
> Funny things he or she will say as she learns to love God
>   and makes new discoveries,
> Record of important dates and experiences,
> And the story of how they come to know Jesus as their
>   personal Savior and so much more.

What a precious treasure she will have. But it gets better. Just imagine when her children are grown and starting out on their own—she will be able to present them with a personalized Bible filled with the legacy of God's faithfulness in their lives up to that point. What a firm foundation to send along with them as they go off to college or to a new career.

I have started another Journaling Bible for the daughter of one of my dearest friends that is getting married later this year. Her mother and I have selected scriptures that will be encouraging to her and her new husband as they start their life together. We have talked about having a "Journaling Shower" for her – where the shower guests would all participate in adding to the Bride and Groom's new family Bible. I think it would be a really unique celebration.

There really is no limit to the ways that you can share your heART in a very personal way. Your gift, could be the start of something incredible . . . perhaps influencing a whole generation! Think outside the box. Who could you bless with a gift of your heART?

My heART's Blessing For You

I can't say good-bye without praying once more over you.

> *Heavenly Father,*
> *I pray and lay hold of Your promise that "no eye has seen, nor ear heard, nor the heart of man imagined, what [You] have prepared for those who love [You]."[58] Bless this dear one. Let them feel Your pleasure when they meet with You on the pages of Your Word. Make it come alive in their hearts. Refresh their spirits and their minds when they see and remember Your lessons. Forge new paths in their minds and lead them to new discoveries of all that You have done on their behalf.*
>
> *Thank You for sending Your Son to die for them!*
> *Thank You for leaving Your Spirit to live in them!*

Thank You for allowing me to touch them on Your behalf. I know how much You love them . . . and there they are loving You right back with all of their heART.

Amen

Resources

This is a collection of all sorts of things that did not fit nicely elsewhere:

- Tools and Supplies
- To Seal or Not To Seal
- Color Gallery
- Journaling Bible Versions
- Facebook Groups To Check Out
- Pinterest Search Terms
- Instagram Hashtags
- Workshops and Tutorials
- Line Art
- Margin Templates
- Contact Information
- God's Plan of Salvation
- End Notes

Tools and Supplies

One of the things I love the most about introducing new artists to *Illuminated Journaling* is that you don't have to make a huge investment in tools and supplies to get started.

However, here are a few basics that you will want to have in your supply drawer as a beginner.

Mechanical Pencil (.07 or .05)

White Eraser

Clear Ruler

Permanent Black Ink Pens-I prefer Micron pens by Sakura. [Nib sizes: 03, 05, 1]

White Gel Pen- I prefer Sakura White Classic Gel

Watercolor Palette – My recommendation is for you to not get the cheapest that is available, because it is just harder to get the results you want. What makes these palettes not work so well is the fact that they don't have much pigment in them and dry very pale and take lots of extra layers just to build up a bit of color on the page. A good low-end watercolor palette is manufactured by Loew-Cornell. They have good pigmentation for the price and are readily available at most craft stores.

Colored Pencils—again, these can be inexpensive.

Graphite Paper

Tracing Paper

I always recommend starting with mid quality – student grade products. After you've practiced a bit, you will know which techniques you use the most – and can begin to upgrade to a bit higher quality of things like your watercolors and your colored pencils.

I almost always use watercolors and colored pencils on my Journaling pages– so I have begun to use highly pigmented products .but that doesn't necessarily mean they are super expensive. I am willing to invest a bit more so that I can be confident how they will look on my Bible pages. Here are the products I recommend for more advanced journalers.

Additional nib sizes of black marker.[.005 and brush]
Upgrade watercolor pallet to Koi or Kuretake
Upgrade pencils, I prefer Prismacolor Premier
Gamsol/Odorless Mineral Spirits (for blending your
colored pencils.
Blending Stumps
Heat tool
Clear Gesso – the only one I really like is Prima's Art
Basics Clear Gesso
OR, Matte Gel Medium

Products that are fun to experiment with:

Distress Inks (you must seal the page)
Pitt Big Brush Pens
Faber-Castell Gelatos
Heavy Body Acrylic Paint
Alphabet and Image Stamps
Archival Ink (permanent ink)

. I have links to most of these products on
IlluminatedJournaling.com:

To Seal Or Not To Seal

Life is filled with mysteries and things that are "unknowable" – but this doesn't have to be one of them.

The paper used in Bibles is thin to keep the weight down. It is also almost always treated with something to help it resist dirt and oil from all of the handling that the pages will get. This can actually work in your favor- depending on what kind of product you are going to be using on your page.

Here are my simple guidelines:

Seal your page with Clear Gesso or Matte Gel Medium if:
1. You are a slow writer. The longer your nib is on the paper the more likely your pen is to soak through.
2. You are using wet mediums like dye inks (slow drying inks) or gelatos or spray inks.
3. You are going to use juicy markers.

You don't need to seal your page if:
1. You are going to use watercolors first.
2. You are only going to be using colored pencils.

Not so complicated, right? I'm not sure what the scientific explanation is – but if you are planning to use watercolors washes – you will be fine with not sealing your page. The very best way to be confident that you will get the results you want is to *test, test, test*!

Now go forth and seal appropriately.

Color Gallery

It is impossible to include all of the journal pages used in the book as illustrations here in the *Color Gallery*—so I have chosen a few that I hope will inspire you – as well as some that did not find a home in one of the chapters. If you would like to see a complete collection of these pages, they are available at: www.IlluminatedJournaling.com

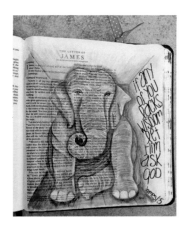

Zechariah 2:8, *Pray for Israel*
Watercolor and colored pencils

Exodus 15:26, *Names of God*
Watercolor and colored pencils

Joshua 4:6,*Stones of Remembrance*
Watercolor and colored pencils

Psalms 1 *Tarry In the Word*
Watercolor and colored pencils

Psalm 40:2, *He Drew Me Up*
Watercolor and colored pencils

Proverbs 22:1, *Good Name*
Watercolor and colored pencils

Habakuk 1:5 *Look!*
Micron Pens and colored pencils

Proverbs 16:24 *Kind Words*
Micron Pen and colored pencils

Titus *Poured Out Richly and Justified by Grace*
Watercolor and colored pencils

Psalm 98:1 *Marvelous Things*
Watercolor and colored pencils

Proverbs 9:10, *Beginning of Wisdom*
Gelatos and colored pencils

John 15:13, *Greater Love*
Watercolor and colored pencils

Ephesians 1 and Ephesians 2:8,
I Am and *For By Grace*
Watercolor and colored pencils

Philippians 1 and Philippians 3:18
I Need Christ and *Yesterday Ended Last Night*
Watercolor and colored pencils

Matthew 6:27 *Single Hour*
Watercolor and colored pencils

Psalm 126:3, *Great Things*
Watercolor and colored pencils

Journaling Bible Versions

While I am sure that there are translations of the Bible that do not come in a Journaling friendly version, I have found a wide range of publishers that have seized the opportunity to provide a wide margin option for their customers. This is not an exhaustive list – but does include the most popular request from people attending my workshops. Most publishers also offer a variety of styles – so if you have a strong preference, keep searching. I have found that by going directly to the publishers website I can determine what options are available – and then use Amazon, ChristianBook.com or Christian Book Distributors to find the best deal on the version you prefer. One more note: Use all three search terms (Journaling Bible, Wide Margin Bible and Notetaker's Bible) as it seems that publishers use these terms interchangeably and without any consistent application of a features.

Amplified (Notetakers/Wide Margin)
Broadman Holman (Journaling Bible)
Catholic: Cambridge NRSV (Wide Margin)
            Oxford NRSV (Notetakers)
English Standard Version ESV (Journaling/ Wide Margin
King James Notetakers
Living Translation – Notetakers
Message –Notetakers
New American Standard Bible (Wide Margin)
New International Version NIV (Notetakers/Wide Margin)
New King James (Wide Margin/Notetakers)
New Living Translation (Wide Margin)

Facebook Groups for Bible Journaling

There are many groups that are focused on Bible Journaling. Some are closed group – which just means that the hosts are trying to provide a safe environment for people to share and be inspired. If you wish to join a group – send a request to the administrator and they will advise you when you have been approved. When you first join a Journaling Group, it is wise to read any information they have published about the guidelines for participation. This will just help you know how best to share what you have been working on in your Bible.

This is not a complete list – just a few that I either participate in or know the leadership personally. To find these groups, simple do a search when you are logged in to Facebook

Bible Art Journaling Challenge (Rebekah Jones)

Creating In Faith (Jamie Dougherty)

Creative Bible Study (Deborah Boutwell)

His Kingdom Come (Shonna Bucaroff)

Illuminated Journaling Workshop (Jann Gray: This group is for my students in my live and online *Illuminated Journaling* Workshops**)**
Illustrated Faith Teens (Shanna Noel)

Journaling Bible Community (Shanna Noel)

Pinterest™ Search Terms

I have found Pinterest™ to be one of my favorite places to go get a bit of "instant inspiration." The first place I look is on my own "boards." I go there first because I know I have already added things that sparked an idea or a technique I want to try. I mention that only because there are two ways to use Pinterest and both are equally good.

1. You do a search and find some inspiration that matches what you are looking for – and depending on what the Pin leads to, you may find a blog or a website with additional resources. This type of search is ideal for when you are looking for something specific.

2. You can set aside some time every few days to go and see what other people have "pinned." If you like what you see – add it to your own boards so that you can easily "put you hands on it" when you have time to try it for yourself. One thing to be aware of – it is easy to get caught up in the "finding inspiration step" and never actually take action on the inspiration. So let me encourage you—if you find something that sparks an idea for you – try and work it into your journaling time as soon as you can.

Search Terms I Use Regularly

Believe	Bible Verse Reference
Biblical Art	Christ
Bible Clip Art	Clip Art
Bible Journaling	Cross/Crosses

Devotional	Faith Images
Faith	Prayer
Faith Art	Ministry
Jesus	Praise
Jesus/Words of	Worship

Add your own:

Instagram Hashtags

#BibleJournaling
#BibleArtChallenge
#BibleArt
#CreatingInFaith
#DivineArt
#DocumentedFaith
#FaithJournaling
#IlluminatedJournaling
#IlluminatedFaith
#IllustratedFaith
#PraiseArt
#DocumentedFaith

Add your own:

Line Art

One of the quickest ways to get started in your Journaling Bible is to use Line Art to get the basic shape onto your page. Here are a few pieces of Line Art to get you started. You can use a copier to resize them to your preference. You can then use a combination of tracing paper and graphite paper to trace and transfer the image onto your page.

Do a "press check" to see how hard you will need to press to get a good transfer and then follow these simple instructions:

1. Temporarily tape your image (on your tracing paper) to your page with some repositionable tape (like Washi tape).
2. Place graphite paper between your image and the page.
3. Use a ball point pen or a stylus to transfer the lines
4. Color and make it your own.

Celtic Cross

Jar from Broken and Spilled Out

Stones from Stones of Remembrance

Flowers from *The Word of the Lord Endures Forever*

Hearts

Blossoms

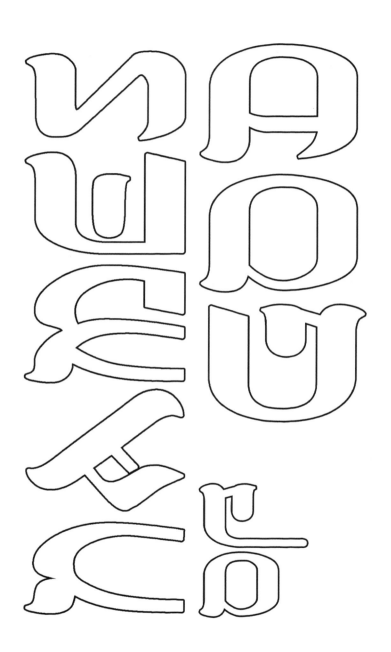

JEHOVAH

JIREH

RAPHA

SHAMMAH

SHALOM

NISSI

RAAH

TSIDKEU

Download this design from
Jamie Dougherty visit:
http://www.mediafire.com/view/kd
7hbasdz64fzpw/Heart.jpg

THE
HOLY BIBLE

2015 Jamie Dougherty Designs

Workshops and Tutorials

What the difference between Workshops and Tutorials?

Great question!

Tutorials. I create tutorials because I love sharing what I have learned while working in my own Bible and Journals. They tend to be on whatever I am working on right now - or sharing a particular technique that people have been curious about after seeing something that I have done. These are free and you can access them on IlluminatedJournaling.com. If you want to be informed as soon as I put a new tutorial up, please subscribe to my YouTube Channel/Jann Gray. I have more than 200 tutorial videos available...and while most of them focus on mixed media and card making, many of the techniques that I share will work in your Bible as well...they may even inspire you to try some new things too!

These are totally free.

Workshops. I have created an ***Illuminated Journaling Workshop Basics*** series to help provide new Journalers with good basic information to make "*starting*" much easier and to help journalers discover their preferred style of creative response to God's Word.

You can also participate in the ***Illuminated Journaling Skills Series*** which are technique focused Workshops to help you add new skills to your journaling toolbox. Workshops are a combination of teaching and demonstration...and are what I would share if I were doing a live classroom event.

Workshops are self-paced and will be available for as long as the website is active. You can take your time, come back and re-watch any session or lesson that you have registered for as many times as you like. If you want to be the first to hear about new classes and workshops, sign up for the Illuminated Journaling Newsletter on the website.

Illuminated Journaling Live: While I thoroughly enjoy preparing and teaching on-line classes – my very favorite way to teach is where I can interact with participants in a live Workshop setting. I am available to come and teach a several session Workshop at an art or scrapbooking supply store, a ministry retreat or as an extracurricular class for Christian Academies. If you would be interested in me teaching in your area, please send me an email via the website. I would love to have that opportunity.

God's Plan Of Salvation

START YOUR NEW LIFE WITH CHRIST

You can have real, lasting peace today through a relationship with Jesus Christ. *Start your four-step journey now!*

Step One—God loves you and has a plan for you.

The Bible says, "God so loved the world that He gave His one and only Son, [Jesus Christ], that whoever believes in Him shall not perish, but have eternal life" (John 3:16).

Jesus said, "I came that they may have life and have it abundantly"—a complete life full of purpose (John 10:10).

But here's the problem:

Step Two—Man is sinful and separated from God.

We have all done, thought or said bad things, which the Bible calls "sin." The Bible says, "All have sinned and fall short of the glory of God" (Romans 3:23).

The result of sin is death, spiritual separation from God (Romans 6:23).

The good news?

Step Three—God sent His Son to die for your sins.

Jesus died in our place so we could have a relationship with God and be with Him forever.

"God demonstrates His own love toward us, in that while we were yet sinners, Christ died for us" (Romans 5:8).

But it didn't end with His death on the cross. He rose again and still lives!

"Christ died for our sins. ... He was buried. ... He was raised on the third day, according to the Scriptures" (1 Corinthians 15:3-4).

Jesus is the only way to God. Jesus said, "I am the way, and the truth, and the life; no one comes to the Father, but through Me" (John 14:6).

Step Four—Would you like to receive God's forgiveness?

We can't earn salvation; we are saved by God's grace when we have faith in His Son, Jesus Christ. All you have to do is believe you are a sinner, that Christ died for your sins, and ask His forgiveness. Then turn from your sins—that's called repentance. Jesus Christ knows you and loves you. What matters to Him is the attitude of your heart, your honesty. We suggest praying the following prayer to accept Christ as your Savior:

"Dear Lord Jesus,
I know I am a sinner, and I ask for your forgiveness. I believe you died for my sins and rose from the dead. I trust and follow you as my Lord and Savior. Guide my life and help me to do your will.
In your name, Amen."

Margin Templates

Use these templates to sketch out ideas and practice new techniques. Remember the paper here in the book is different than that in your Bible, but you can gain confidence by trying things here first!

NOTES:

NOTES:

NOTES:

NOTES:

NOTES:

NOTES:

NOTES:

NOTES:

NOTES:

NOTES:

NOTES:

NOTES:

NOTES:

NOTES:

NOTES:

NOTES:

NOTES:

NOTES:

NOTES:

NOTES:

NOTES:

:

NOTES:

NOTES:

NOTES:

NOTES:

:

NOTES:

NOTES:

NOTES:

NOTES:

NOTES:

NOTES:

NOTES:

NOTES:

NOTES:

NOTES:

Let's Stay In Touch

I want to stay in touch and I hope you do too!

Please sign up for the *Illuminated Journaling Newsletter* as I will be sending out an occasional newsletter - when I have new workshops or resources to announce. It's easy to do on the website and that is the best way to be up-to-date on everything going on with *Illuminated Journaling*.

I would love to hear from you... feel free to contact me at Jann@janngray.com! I get some of my best inspiration from you...so don't hesitate to let me know how I can help you!

Finally, if you would like to book me for a live event, please contact:

Royce Gray: 615-773-1234

End Notes and Bibliography

[1] Eric Liddell, Christian and Olympic Gold Runner, 1924 Summer Olympic Games. **Chariots of Fire.**

[2] Matthew 2:13-15 ESV Journaling Bible pg. 808 *Joseph Knew God's Voice,* journaling entry by Jann Gray.

[3] James 1:5 ESV Journaling Bible pg. 1011 *The Elephant In The Room,* journaling entry by Jann Gray.

[4] Psalm 90:2 ESV Journaling Bible pg. 496 *From Everlasting to Everlasting,* and Jeremiah 29:11 ESV Journaling Bible pg. 656 *The Plans I Have For You* journaling entry by Jann Gray.

\g[5] Isaiah 40:8 ESV Journaling Bible pg. 597 *The Word Endures Forever,* journaling entry by Jann Gray.

[6] 1 Corinthians 10:23-24 New International Version, Zondervan Publishing.

[7] http://www.imdb.com/title/tt0082158/quotes

[8] Philippians 2:13 ESV Journaling Bible pgs. 981-982 *Feel His Pleasure.*

[9] Psalm 139:14, ESV Journaling Bible, page 522

[10] Romans 1:19,20 ESV Journaling Bible, page 939

[11] Genesis 9:16 ESV Journaling Bible, page 7 *See and Remember.*

[12] Genesis 9:16 ESV Journaling Bible, page 7

[13] (c) Lisa Pemberton, Facebook. Link to article: http://www.dailymail.co.uk/news/article-2030826/Tearjerker-Loyal-dog-lay-Navy-SEAL-masters-coffin-funeral-football-mascot-soldiers-home-state.html#ixzz3YvHodBkH

[14] *Yesterday Ended Last Night*, ESV Journaling Bible, page 981

[15] Lamentations 3:22,23, ESV Journaling Bible page 688

[16] Philippians 3:13,14 ESV Journaling Bible page 981

[17] Psalm 121:1,2 ESV Journaling Bible page 516.

[18] Joshua 4:6-7 ESV Journaling Bible, page 180 *Stones of Remembrance*

[19] **Turn, Turn, Turn** *The Byrds,* http://www.metrolyrics.com/turn-turn-turn-lyrics-the-byrds.html

[20] Matthew 22:37 ESV Journaling Bible, page 828 *Love the Lord.*
[21] Titus 3:5-7 ESV Journaling Bible, page 999 *Justified By Grace.*
[22] 1 Corinthians 1:4-7, ESV Journaling Bible page 952. *You Are Not Lacking Any Gift.*
[23] Zechariah 2:8 ESV Journaling Bible page 793 *Pray for Israel.*
[24] Psalm 128:3 ESV Journaling Bible page 16 *Trust In The Lord*
[25] Jeremiah 29:11 ESV Journaling Bible page 656 *Hope and a Future.*
[26] Philippians ESV Journaling Bible page 980 *I Need Christ.*
[27] Proverbs 3:9-10 ESV Journaling Bible page 528.
[28] Link in Resource Section to on-line version of the "Art of Tracing" workshop called "Working With Line Art."
[29] L.M. Montgomery, *Anne of Green Gables*
[30] 2 Chronicles 20:15 ESV Journaling Bible page 372.
[31] Spring 2012 issue of Lapham's Quarterly, *Means of Communication.*
[32] Psalm 126:3 ESV Journaling Bible page 518 *The Lord Has Done Great Things*
[33] britishlibrary.typepad.co.uk the St Omer Psalter (c. 1330-1340, BL Yates Thompson MS 14)
[34] James 1:5 ESV Journaling Bible page1011.
[35] 2 Kings 2:23-24 ESV Journaling Bible page 308
[36] Ephesians 2:8 ESV Journaling Bible page 977. *Your Grace.*
[37] Ephesians 1:3-6 ESV Journaling Bible page 976. *I Am.*
[38] 1 Corinthians 14:33 ESV Journaling Bible page 961
[39] Isaiah 40:8 ESV Journaling Bible page 599 *The Word Endures Forever.*
[40] I know I almost lost you there because your brain just went scurrying down another pat . . . *"sealer? I need sealer? Where do I get that? Oh good grief, I could have ruined my Bible!"* See my article on sealing your pages in the Resource section.
[41] © 2015 Jamie Dougherty Designs.
[42] http://www.thinkingcloset.com/2015/04/03/permission-pages-a-perfectionists-approach-to-the-journaling-bible/
[43] © 2014 *Shake It Off* by Taylor Swift. Album **1989**.

[44] Isaiah 65:4 ESV Journaling Bible page 623 *Dream God Sized Dreams.*.

[45] Nehemiah ESV Journaling Bible page 398 *O Lord!*

[46] John 19 ESV Journaling Bible page 905 *It's Friday But Sunday's Coming.*

[47] Isaiah 43:4 ESV Journaling Bible page 603

[48] Psalm 91:14 ESV Journaling Bible page 497

[49] Romans 5:6-8 ESV Journaling Bible page 942

[50] John 3:16 ESV Journaling Bible page 888 *Whoever Believes.*

[51] Isaiah 49:16 ESV Journaling Bible page 610. *Inscribed On His Palms.*

[52] 2 Corinthians 6:18 ESV Journaling Bible page 967

[53] Luke 10: 38-42 ESV Journaling Bible page 869. John 12:1-8 ESV Journaling Bible page 898. *Broken and Spilled Out.*

[54] Isaiah 55:11 ESV Journaling Bible page 616.

[55] Matthew 7:6 ESV Journaling Bible page 812.

[56] 1 Chronicles 4:10 ESV Journaling Bible pages 336-337 *Prayer of Jabez.*

[57] Revelation 21:5 ESV Journaling Bible page 1041 *All Things New.*

[58] 1 Corinthians 2:9 ESV Journaling Bible page 953.